So... What's a Tutor to Do?

Cathy M. Roller

University of Iowa
Iowa City, Iowa, USA

INTERNATIONAL Reading Association

800 Barksdale Road, PO Box 8139
Newark, Delaware 19714-8139, USA
www.reading.org

The International Reading Association attempts, through its publications, to provide a forum for a wide spectrum of opinions on reading. This policy permits divergent viewpoints without implying the endorsement of the Association.

Director of Publications   Joan M. Irwin
Managing Editor, Books and Electronic Publications   Christian A. Kempers
Associate Editor   Matthew W. Baker
Assistant Editor   Janet S. Parrack
Assistant Editor   Mara P. Gorman
Publications Coordinator   Beth Doughty
Association Editor   David K. Roberts
Production Department Manager   Iona Sauscermen
Graphic Design Coordinator   Boni Nash
Electronic Publishing Supervisor   Wendy A. Mazur
Electronic Publishing Specialist   Anette Schütz-Ruff
Electronic Publishing Specialist   Cheryl J. Strum
Electronic Publishing Assistant   Peggy Mason

Library of Congress Cataloging in Publication Data
   Roller, Cathy M.
   So what's a tutor to do? / Cathy M. Roller.
      p.   cm.
   Includes bibliographical references and index.
   1. Reading (Primary).   2. Tutors and tutoring.   3. Reading teachers.   I. Title.
LB1525.L6256   1998   98-14427
371.4'—dc21
ISBN 0-87207-191-X (pbk.)

Contents

Introduction

We Can Do It Right

EVERY CHILD *[in the United States] will be able to read by the end of third grade.* U.S. President Bill Clinton announced this goal in his State of the Union Address on January 20, 1997. The Reading Corps he proposed will use volunteers to provide individualized tutoring for children in Kindergarten through Grade 3 who want and need it. A U.S. Department of Education document describing the president's initiative provides clear examples of what it means to read by third grade and suggests specific books that children should be able to read and understand. It cites research evidence that tutoring is effective and describes some characteristics of successful tutoring programs.

President Clinton issued a bold challenge. We can meet that challenge, but we must do it right. What the brief Department of Education document does not emphasize is that tutoring programs vary dramatically in their effectiveness (Cohen, Kulik, & Kulik, 1982). It also does not indicate

- that highly prescribed tutoring programs (those that tell tutors exactly what to do) are generally better than those that are less prescribed;
- that tutoring in math is generally more effective than tutoring in reading;
- that programs evaluated using word pronunciation and factual questions show more gains than programs evaluated using higher level comprehension questions;
- that programs in which tutors give hints to help tutees solve their own problems are more effective than those in which the tutor provides answers;

1

- that tutors who demonstrate and explain strategies are more effective than tutors who do not demonstrate and explain;

- that more complete tutoring programs are generally more effective than those that focus on a single aspect of reading; and

- that programs including sound-awareness training are generally more effective than those that do not.

Researchers and teachers know a lot about tutoring children: The purpose of this book is to acquaint you with that knowledge and help you put it to good use.

Much of this book is based on my experience with the summer reading clinic that is part of the University of Iowa Summer Residential Program (SRP). I have written about the SRP morning classroom in *Variability Not Disability: Struggling Readers in a Workshop Classroom* (Roller, 1996). *Variability Not Disability* focuses on classroom instruction. *So ...What's a Tutor to Do?* looks at the individual tutoring sessions that are an integral part of the SRP program. I will refer the reader to chapters in *Variability Not Disability* that contain useful information for tutors.

The sessions described in this book are based on those led by graduate students seeking certification in reading and special education, who tutor the SRP children and attend a daily lecture as part of their master's degree programs. They are observed regularly by supervisors who provide feedback. Every tutoring session is recorded on a cassette player and tutors listen to the tapes to evaluate their own teaching. They also transcribe short sections of these tapes as part of their course requirements. In 1996 I tutored lesson segments in place of the graduate tutors and taped the graduate student tutors on either the day before or after I taught. Most of the examples in this book are drawn from my tapes and those of the graduate students.

Although this book is intended for tutors, it will be most effective if used under the direction of a qualified reading specialist. Reading instruction is very complex and no book can hope to tell tutors everything they need to know. Good reading instruction requires volunteers trained under the supervision of a reading specialist. The sections at the end of each chapter labeled "For the Supervisor" will help this reading professional anticipate some of the difficulties that volunteer tutors may encounter.

A great deal has been learned in our program and others like it throughout the United States about tutoring children in reading. The president has called on us to meet his reading challenge by developing a reading corps of trained tutors led by reading experts. I hope this book will help in this training and in so doing help every child in the United States learn to read by the third grade.

Chapter 1

Where to Begin: What Do Tutoring Sessions Look Like?

TUTORING IS *difficult, and you may have no idea where to begin or what a tutoring session looks like*. What is covered in sessions? How much time is spent on each section? What is my role as a tutor? This chapter will describe tutoring sessions with three different kinds of early readers. Its purpose is to provide an overview. Do not expect to understand every detail; there will be a full chapter devoted to each activity later in the book. For now you should read to get an overall impression of the kinds of things that tutors and children do during tutoring sessions.

ACTIVITIES IN THE TUTORING SESSION

Most reading tutoring sessions last about 30 to 45 minutes and include several basic activities: (1) reading easy books to build confidence; (2) reading new books that include a few challenges; (3) a writing activity; (4) a minilesson about words, word-recognition strategies, comprehension strategies, or other critical skills; and (5) reading challenging books. SRP tutoring sessions, as well as Success For All (Wasik & Slavin, 1983) and Reading Recovery (Handerhan, 1990), two other successful tutoring programs, spend over half the tutoring sessions actually reading books.

3

Reading easy books is just what it sounds like. This activity gives readers the opportunity to read fluently and well. The books should be easy enough for the child to read without help, and the goal should be to enjoy the book. In general, reading easy books means allowing the child to choose a book that they read to you. You may want to talk briefly about the book, either before, during, or after the reading.

Reading the new book is the activity in which most new learning occurs. The new book is one that the child can read relatively well; however, it includes a few challenges so that the child can learn new strategies, skills, and words with the help of the tutor. This activity is important and more tutoring time should be spent on it than on any other.

Writing is included in the tutoring session because reading and writing are closely related and information learned in one activity can be reinforced with the other activity. In tutoring sessions where time with the tutor is necessarily brief, writing activities cannot be very extensive. However, a few well-chosen writing activities directed specifically at what the child needs to learn can promote learning.

Minilessons are specific and direct lessons that focus on something important the child needs to learn. Tutors know what the child needs to learn because as they are reading and writing with the child, they pay attention to what the child knows and what he or she is ready to learn next. Chapter 11 includes lists of sample minilessons. Although these lessons are brief, they are effective because they can be targeted accurately to the individual child's learning needs.

Reading challenging books is included in the tutoring session because many children who struggle with learning to read feel as though they never get a chance to read "good" books. "Good" books have words that are too hard for them. It is important for children to have the opportunity to read books that they actually want to read and the one-on-one tutoring session is an excellent place to read challenging books because the tutor is there to give needed support. Reading challenging books is one way to remind the child of what their struggle is all about—reading good books. Its inclusion in tutoring boosts children's motivation.

Basic activities in reading tutoring sessions are similar across programs because the best way to learn to read is to learn about reading as you are reading. Tutorial sessions that include reading easy books, reading new books, and reading challenging books ensure that children will have many opportunities to read. Using these in a single tutorial session means a first-grade child may read four or five short books. This is many more pages and words than an average first-grade struggling reader reads daily during school instruction (Allington, 1983). This abundance of reading is a very important part of what makes tutoring effective.

Having provided a quick description of the activities that make up a tutoring session, I will now give an overview of tutoring activities for emergent, beginning, and transition readers. First, however, I will describe each type of reader.

THE THREE CATEGORIES OF EARLY READERS

Emergent readers are really prereaders. They are learning basic print concepts including the idea that words consist of letters representing sounds, that print moves from the top to the bottom of the page and from left to right, and that print conveys a message. They recognize only a few words and need the support of familiar or patterned text (text that repeats sentences over and over, changing just one or two words with each repetition) and strong pictures in order to read.

Beginning readers know a lot about reading. They understand how print works and they have at least 100 to 300 words they know instantly. They can use sounds and letters to identify some words, and they have several strategies to use when they come to words they do not know. For example, they may read on to get more context and then go back to the word, or they may use the letters to try and sound it out. Beginning readers must learn to coordinate all of this information and put it to work as they read.

Instruction for transition readers involves shifting emphases because they read less orally and more silently. They also read fewer picture books and more chapter books, and fewer narrative books and more expository books that present information to be learned. Because they do more silent reading, their instruction includes less emphasis on word identification and more focus on comprehension. The transition reader has mastered basic word-identification skills and is ready to use reading for enjoyment and learning.

The sections that follow provide an example of each of the basic activities for emergent, beginning, and transition readers, and Figures 1, 2, and 5 summarize the basic activities for these three reader types. The characteristics of these three types of readers are summarized in Table 2 on page 48. Remember, the point of this chapter is not to teach you how to do the activities, but rather to give you a quick overview and an idea of what tutoring is like. Each of the activities has a full chapter devoted to them later in the book.

EMERGENT READERS

Reading Easy Books

Because emergent readers are just developing their notions of reading, they need the experience of reading well. Simple books with patterned sentences and explicit picture cues for words not repeated in the pattern help emergent readers read fluently. For example, a book may repeat the pattern _____ *lives in a* _____, with each page containing a clear picture of the animal and the home mentioned on that page. Choice of book is critical to the success of easy reading. The important thing to remember is that the child should not need help to read the book.

Jason is an older (nearly fifth-grade) reader who has struggled mightily to learn to read. He has an average IQ but has a great deal of difficulty actually hearing the sounds in words despite his extensive instruction in sound awareness and phonics. We do not know exactly why Jason has this problem, but recent brain research suggests that for some struggling readers, a certain part of the brain that is responsible for hearing the sounds in words does not always function the way it does for most readers. Jason knows only a few words and seems to use mostly beginning letters when he is trying to figure out words he does not know.

I was Jason's teacher for one of his tutoring sessions. The book we used was *Here Comes the Cat* (Asch, 1989). It contains only the four words included in the title. I chose this book after watching the previous day's tutoring session. Jason had been angry, sullen, and defiant because he could not read the books the tutor was using. I wanted to be *sure* he could read the book. *Here Comes the Cat* has great illustrations and a surprise ending. I thought Jason might like it because I had enjoyed it when I read it the day before.

I began our session with a pep talk and showed him the progress he had made since the previous school year. Because I wanted Jason to succeed, I did not assume that he knew all four words, asking instead, "Which ones do you know?" He knew all four, and read, "Here comes the cat" each time it appeared in print. He used good expression and varied the way he said the sentence, a fact I pointed out, saying, "I like it when you say it like that. I'm sure that's the way they'd say it." We talked about why everyone in the book was running around; Jason said they were running around because they were mice. When he finished reading, we discussed the surprise ending. The final pictures showed the cat bringing cheese for the mice. The mice were not afraid of the cat; they were excited because they wanted the cheese.

My session with Jason illustrates how to use easy books with emergent readers; sessions with younger children look much the same. The key feature of easy reading is that it really be easy. The point is enjoyment and practice and teaching should be kept to a minimum. Talk about the meaning of the story should dominate the conversation, and the child should gain confidence and self-respect from reading the stories fluently and well.

Reading the New Book

In the session with Jason described in the previous section, we also read *Tracks* (Williams, 1992b) which is a little harder than *Here Comes the Cat*. Each page shows a set of tracks, and the print says, "Who made these tracks?" The following page contains a picture of the animal or object that made the track and the text identifies the track maker. Like *Here Comes the Cat*, *Tracks* has a surprise ending. This book offered some important instructional opportunities.

We began this segment by introducing the book to Jason. In SRP, we encourage all the children to introduce books to themselves before they read them. For emergent readers this usually means looking at the cover and title and talking about what the book might be about, as well as looking through the pictures and talking about what is happening. The tutor is often very active during the introduction and makes sure to use words that may be difficult for the child to pronounce when discussing the pictures. Because this book was relatively easy for Jason, we looked through the pictures and he actually read some of the pages. At the end, he commented that the last page was kind of funny. The introduction prepared Jason for reading by familiarizing him with the book's subject.

When we began looking at the book Jason read, "What makes these tracks?" instead of "Who made these tracks?" I did not stop him because what he was saying made sense and the beginning letters of the words, "What makes" matched the beginning letters of the text words *Who made*. About four pages into the book Jason stopped and stared at the print. He said, "What makes? Is that right?" I answered, "I like the way you're looking at the print there because you're getting the idea that what you're saying isn't quite right." Then I pointed to *made* and said, "Can this be *makes?*" Jason answered, "No," and then I asked, "What does it end in?" pointing to the *d* in *made* so he would not be confused by the silent *e* at the end. He said, "/d/, *made*." I complimented him and he said, "How made?" Because I sensed his growing frustration I said, "OK. This would be *who*." Jason then read, "Who made these tracks?" He finished reading the book with help in just a few more places.

During this reading I kept the focus primarily on the meaning of the book, but at the point where I knew he was ready for it, when he paused and asked if he was saying the word right, I taught about paying attention to the ending sounds during word recognition. This was an important lesson that Jason needed to learn because he was attending to beginning letters and noticing the ends of words is the next developmental step. Notice, however, that I did not stop and teach at every mistake. In fact, I let him read the text incorrectly for several pages because his reading made sense and matched the beginning letters. I only taught when I knew that he was ready for a lesson. Knowing when to teach, when to ignore errors, and when to give the child a word, as I did with *who*, is part of what tutors need to learn (see Chapters 4 and 9 for further discussion of knowing when to teach).

Writing

Jason and his regular tutor, Martha, were alternating turns as they wrote every other page of a book about dogs. They began one writing lesson with Jason reading all the pages they had written thus far. Jason had good ideas for his pages and wrote "Dogs are fun to play with" on one page and "I go swimming with my dog" on another. Jason wrote his sentences on scratch paper first, then he and Martha edited them and wrote them in the book. His scratch paper spellings were not always correct, but Martha let him complete his sentences first and then worked with him to edit what he had written.

During editing Jason was not sure of the vowel in *wet*. Martha gave him several choices but he was still unsure so she said, "*E* is the best choice." At another point she helped him with *shakes* by first saying the word very slowly, and then having him say the word slowly and write down the sounds he heard. He was able to spell it. Jason asked if he could take his book home toward the end of the session and Martha said yes.

This lesson demonstrates three important principles to follow during writing: First, spelling is not a focus in draft writing. Second, spelling does become a focus during the editing process when the point is to make everything perfect so that it is ready for other readers. It is important to note here that for some younger readers perfection may not be necessary because adults are accustomed to tolerating and even enjoying the invented spellings and mistakes of young children. However, perfection is important for older children who have experienced a lot of failure and who have come to hate writing. They do not need to have their mistakes criticized by others, adding another failure to those they already have accumulated. At SRP we have the children correct only the parts of their pieces that they can correct easily and quickly. We, as their editors, do the rest. The third principle is that of having a real audience, in Jason's case the other children who lived with him at the dorm for the duration of SRP. Writing for an audience is a very powerful motivator for writing; I will return to this idea later in the book.

Minilessons

During reading and writing lessons, tutors often notice an important piece of information or a strategy that children need to know. For example while reading the new book with Jason, I noted that although he seemed to be attending to beginning sounds in word identification he was not always paying attention to ending sounds. A typical minilesson might begin in the following way:

Tutor: Yesterday when we were reading you first called this word [point to the word written on the dry erase board] *makes*. But after you looked at it, we figured out the word was...

Child: *Made.*

Tutor: That's right, *made*. Why is that the word *made* and not *makes*?

Hopefully the child will be able to talk about the ways the two words end. But if he or she cannot, the tutor then guides the child through the steps of noticing the *k* and *s* sounds at the end of *makes* and the *d* silent *e* at the end of *made*. The tutor then works through a few more examples using other words drawn from the child's reading and writing, demonstrating how this helps when the child reads.

Tutor: Suppose you read this sentence [points to the words "When did he get back home?" on the dry erase board.] "What did he get back home?" and that didn't make sense. You look hard at that first word and you see that there's no *t* on the end. *What* ends in *t* so it can't be *what*. Then you stop and think, "well it ends in *n*—what would makes sense that starts with *w* and ends with *n*? *When*. "When did he get back home?" That makes sense. Paying attention to the ends of words can help you. Now what do I want you to do when you are having trouble figuring out a word?

Jason needed to learn that his reading must make sense and that when it was not making sense, attention to letters would help him figure things out. Early readers usually show a progression of first attending to beginning sounds then to ending sounds—later they attend to the middles of words. Because Jason was already using beginning sounds, I was encouraging him to take the next step and pay attention to ending sounds.

Reading Challenging Books

It is important that children spend a major part of their instructional time reading books that are easy for them and that they can read with just a little assistance. However, it is also important that children's reading not be limited to those kinds of books. Often children cannot read the books they want to read and do not want to read the books they can read. If children are not getting to read books they like, it is important to include challenging books in at least a small segment of session. There are many ways to help children gain access to books that they cannot read themselves (see *Variability Not Disability*, Chapter 4). For emergent readers this probably means reading the book to the child and simply sharing the fun and enjoyment of reading a good book together. The basic guideline is to let the child do what the child can do while the tutor does what the child cannot do. Figure 1 is an overview of tutoring activities for emergent readers.

BEGINNING READER

Reading Easy Books

Mike could identify some words and use strategies to figure out some words he did not know. He needed to learn more words and strategies and to coordinate his knowledge and skills as he read. He was using his easy reading to prepare for reading to small children at a nearby day-care center. Mike gathered several books and told me he was going to let the children choose the one they wanted him to read. Then he began to read *If You Meet A Dragon* (Mesler, 1990) for me:

> If you meet a dragon, tickle his back, tickle his nose, tickle his legs, tickle his toes, tickle his tail, tickle his chin, and that will be the end of him.

Figure 1
Activities for Emergent Readers

Reading Easy Books

1. Child chooses book.
2. Child reads book.
3. Child and tutor talk about book either before, during, or after reading.

Reading the New Book

1. Child chooses book from tutor's selection.
2. Book Introduction
   a. Read title.
   b. Look at cover and predict what it is about.
   c. Look at pictures and talk about story. (Make sure you use words you expect the child to have difficulty with, but leave some work for the child to do.)
3. Child reads the book with tutor's support.

Writing

1. Child decides what he or she wants to write.
2. Child writes draft using temporary spelling.
3. Child and tutor edit the writing.
4. Child writes (or tutor may type) final copy.

Minilesson

1. Tutor introduces the lesson that is based on recent performance of the child.
2. Tutor models and explains.
3. Tutor asks for feedback.
4. Tutor follows up on lesson in actual reading.

Reading Challenging Books

1. Child chooses book.
2. Tutor reads book to child.

He read the book fluently and perfectly, and it was clear that he enjoyed the reading. Notice that this book has more words and is more complex than *Here Comes the Cat*, but is still very simple. It begins with one phrase and ends with another and the middle pages all have *tickle his* _____ with a clear picture cue on the page. In addition there is a rhyme with *nose/toes* and a near rhyme with *chin/him*. Mike was very successful. This is important in the very public situation of reading to children. He practiced this book many times to make sure he could read it, and he was proud of the way he read.

Reading the New Book

Randy was reading *Mushrooms for Dinner* (Randall, 1994). This book is not patterned; however, it is fairly easy because it has simple sentences, a limited number of words that are repeated frequently, and strong pictures that support the story line and help with word identification. We began by discussing the book because Randy's tutor had introduced it the day before. Randy started by reading fairly fluently, "Father Bear came home and said, 'Look. No mushrooms.'" But then he got confused, "I don't know (pause) nnnn (pause) ot I don't not (pause) I did not find any. That doesn't make any sense." By the time he finished reading it, he was so confused that he did not realize his final attempt, "I did not find any," *did* make sense. I responded, "Try it again because you almost got it sensible. [I think what I meant was, 'you almost made it make sense.'] Why don't you start over at the beginning. Sometimes that really helps. And think about what father might be saying." Randy then reread the passage fluently.

He continued reading well and solving any problems he had himself. I intervened at one point to say that it was good that he corrected himself when he read "mushrooms" for *some*, but it would have really been OK to continue without correcting because he was making sense. Toward the end of the book he ran into trouble with *clever* in the sentence, "You are a clever little bear." He hesitated and I encouraged him to keep going and come back to reread. When he reread he kept saying "clooo clooo." I said, "cle," and Randy said, "clever." I did not interrupt the lesson at this point to teach about vowels because the book was very short and the interruption would be long and would destroy the flow of the story.

After he finished reading, I called Randy's attention to *clever* and its meaning. Then I asked him if he knew anything about vowels. He named them immediately, and when I asked him if he knew the sounds he fired off the short vowel sounds, "/a/, /e/, /i/, /o/, /u/" without taking a breath. All the short vowel sounds were correct, including the short /e/ sound that he had not spontaneously used to figure out *clever*. Although *clever* is a confusing word that might be pronounced with either a long or short vowel sound, using either of the /e/ sounds would have made more sense than the long /o/ sound that Randy had tried. I asked him if he thought about vowel sounds when he was trying to figure out *clever*. He had not. I said, "Vowels can help you when you're stuck. You were going cloooooo, but there's no /o/ there. There's an /e/ sound, 'clever.'" He made the short /e/ sound and said "clever." And I said, "So you can use your vowels to help you too." I also had him write *clever* to increase the probability that he would remember it the next time he saw it.

We concluded the activity with me complimenting Randy on the progress he had made over the course of time he had spent in SRP. Randy knew a lot about reading, but he could not yet use all that he knew automatically and spontaneously as he read.

Writing

With beginning readers, writing, like reading, is a matter of coordination. Children often know more about writing than they can demonstrate because getting all their knowledge ordered and functioning is difficult for them.

Randy was excited about a sports car called the Dodge Viper. His tutor prepared a blank book with illustrations he had drawn or selected from brochures. Randy was writing text to go with the illustrations.

I came in for a writing session that was devoted to editing the book. Randy first read his text to me. As he was reading, he noted that there was something wrong with the word *shope [shape]*. When he finished I asked him to circle all the words that were spelled correctly and to underline those spelled incorrectly. He was very accurate, and in the end we worked on spelling *shape* and *Viper*. He correctly identified the vowel sound in *shape* as an /a/ rather than an /o/, and he changed *Vipen* to *Viper*, correctly hearing the ending /r/.

As with all readers, beginning readers should first focus on the content of their writing. Encouraging children to use temporary spellings in drafts is important, because emphasizing spelling too early may result in their using only words they know how to spell. The number of words they can spell is much more limited than the words they know so emphasizing spelling early in the writing process restricts the content of what struggling readers write. The temporary spelling also offers opportunities to reinforce and teach how letters and sounds go together.

Because writing is hard work for beginning readers, it is often helpful to construct a set of illustrations first as Randy's tutor did. The illustrations help the child follow the story line and the information in the story, and make coordinating information easier.

Minilessons

Minilessons also are determined by the child's needs. For example, when reading *Mushrooms for Dinner* Randy used an inappropriate vowel sound in his attempt to pronounce *clever*. Because *clever* is a regular word and has the short /e/ sound as in *Ed*, some direct instruction on *using* short vowel sounds might be appropriate, especially because Randy clearly knew what the short vowel sounds were. The lesson should be very short and should come in the part of the session reserved for short lessons:

Tutor: Yesterday when we were reading, I noticed that you weren't sure what vowel sound to use in this word [using dry erase board to write *clever*].

Child: Yes....It's *e*, isn't it?

Tutor: How did you know?

Child: I remembered.

Tutor: Good for you. You know *clever* now. Let's write it.

Child: [writes on dry erase board.]

At this point the teacher would quickly review short vowel sounds using some example words that clearly illustrate their sounds (/a/—*apple*, /e/—*Ed*, /i/—*in*, /o/—*octopus*, and /u/—*umbrella*) and then go into a lesson about using vowel sounds to help in word identification—much like the one I gave when explaining that vowels could help in word identification during the reading activity. Because English is tricky, words like *clever*, in which the first vowel is followed by a single consonant and then another vowel, sometimes use the short sound (as in *robin*) and sometimes the long sound (as in *robot*). I might spend some time asking what would happen if we had first tried the long sound for *e* in *clever*. Because it would not make sense, this could reinforce another basic rule: When one strategy is not working try something else.

Minilessons should focus on something the child really needs to know. They should be identified as a short segment for specific lessons and separated from the reading and writing sections of the tutoring session. Minilessons also should include some examples of application. This is important for all readers, but it is particularly important for beginning readers because using all of their knowledge during reading is their major developmental task.

Reading Challenging Books   *Paired reading*

There are several ways to read challenging books with beginning readers. One way is to read them to the child. Another important technique is paired reading (Topping, 1987). In paired reading, the tutor and the child read a book together. The child begins reading and when he or she hesitates or makes a mistake, the tutor waits five seconds, repeats the word until the child says it correctly, and then continues reading together with the child making sure he or she says every word correctly. When the child uses a prearranged signal, such as touching the tutor's arm, to tell the tutor that he or she is ready to read alone, the tutor stops reading.

There are many other ways to share reading, and tutors, parents, and children seem to discover these on their own. Sometimes the child and the tutor alternate turns, with the tutor reading a sentence, paragraph, or a page and the child reading a sentence, paragraph, or a page. Sometimes the tutor and the child read together. Sometimes they reread important segments of the text. The tutor should always let the child do what the child can do and the tutor should do what the child cannot do. Figure 2 provides an example of how to run the tutoring session for beginning readers.

TRANSITION READERS

Reading Easy Books

Margaret chose *Alexander and the Terrible, Horrible, No Good, Very Bad Day* (Viorst, 1972) as her easy reading because she intended to read it to younger children at a day-care center. I was the tutor for this activity. I opened the conversation by saying, "This is a great book. I love Judith Viorst. She writes for adults as well as children. Do you know that this story is about her son? She has a son named Alexander who is all grown up now." Margaret read the book fluently and I joined in with her on the "terrible, horrible, no good, very bad day" parts. At several points in the book I commented on the story, saying things like, "He has a good mind, doesn't he?" Margaret agreed, and I said that he is good at thinking up bad things to happen.

The transition reader can read quite a few books, but it is sometimes difficult to motivate them to read easy books. They are often so proud of reading more difficult books that they spend all their time with them. At SRP we find the practice of send-

---

Figure 2
Activities for Beginning Readers

Reading Easy Books

1. Child chooses book.
2. Child reads book.
3. Child and tutor talk about book either before, during, or after reading.

Reading the New Book

1. Child chooses book from tutor's selection.
2. Book Introduction
   a. Read title.
   b. Look at cover and predict what it is about.
   c. Look at pictures and talk about story.
3. Child reads the book with tutor's support.

Writing

1. Child decides what he or she wants to write.
2. Child writes draft using temporary spelling.
3. Child and tutor edit the writing.
4. Child writes (or tutor may type) final copy.

Minilesson

1. Tutor introduces the lesson which is based on recent performance of the child.
2. Tutor models and explains.
3. Tutor asks for feedback.
4. Tutor follows up on lesson in actual reading.

Reading Challenging Books

1. Child chooses book.
2. Tutor and child read the book together using a comfortable pattern of taking turns. Focus is on enjoying the book and instruction is kept to a minimum.

---

ing older children to read to younger children at a nearby day-care center does motivate easy reading; sometimes we motivate the reading as preparation for sharing or as preparation for a presentation to classmates. Another way to motivate easy reading is to promote rereading to increase reading rate. The children want to read faster and respond well to keeping graphs and charts of their improvement.

Reading the New Book

Trevor chose the book *Beavers Beware!* (Brenner, 1992). He began the session by explaining how he introduces a book to himself. He said he reads the title and the back cover and pages through the book looking at the pictures. We began reading orally, but after several pages I was confident that Trevor had mastered word-identification skills and should begin reading silently. Transition readers need to make the transition to silent reading for several reasons. First, most reading tasks demand silent reading, which therefore is the goal of reading instruction. Second, because the oral reading of struggling readers is usually very weak and invites teacher interruptions, it is better to have them read silently so they can be in control of when they receive help. Good readers must monitor their own reading to recognize when they are having problems that they need to fix. Silent reading provides a better opportunity to develop this skill. Therefore I suggested Trevor read each page silently and then talk with me about what he read. When he completed the first page he retold the story accurately and said he had no problems. At several points we discussed the story. We had a long talk about why beavers' teeth might be orange. Trevor continued to read and retell the story, but I noticed he was trying to recall everything on the page and tell it to me in the exact words of the story. I gave him the following instruction:

> OK now, when you tell me what's on the page you don't have to tell me every word exactly what's on the page. You can kinda interpret it yourself. Like if I were telling you about this, what I would say is, "Um, the little girl ran in and told her parents about the beaver, and then Mom and Dad kind of thought about everything and they remembered the bark, sticks, and the branches, and they decided that there must be beavers building a lodge." So you don't have to just give every word, you just have to think about it and tell what it means to you.

We continued to work on retelling and his tutor continued the procedure in his next session. Trevor was just beginning to change his concept of reading from a laborious word-identification task to a meaning-getting task. Often children who have struggled to learn to read need special attention to meaning at this stage. They are finally beginning to be able to identify words and they are proud of themselves. They like the idea that they can read by themselves and that they can sometimes achieve both accuracy and fluency at the same time. It often takes direct instruction to help the child shift focus from words to meaning.

Writing

Writing with transition readers is often a matter of getting out of the child's way. One tutor asked me to come in and teach a writing segment of the lesson because she could not get the child to write. I had watched a part of the previous lesson, and I noticed that the tutor was sitting very close to her student, Emma, and asking questions the whole time. When I went in the next day, I showed Emma a "bubble technique." (See Figures 3 and 4.)

I demonstrated for Emma, saying the following:

> Sometimes what I do is I start out like this with a bubble that says what I'm going to write about—say my SRP day. Then I decide some little bubbles would be very helpful and I make little bubbles to remind me what I'm going to say. So like if I was gonna write about my SRP day—this would be Dr. Roller's SRP day. In the small bubbles I'm going to put morning walk, watching morning sessions, responding to papers and college class at lunch.

After explaining and showing Emma how I did this, I helped her make a bubble chart for her topic. We then both wrote for 7 or 8 minutes, finishing the activity by reading our pieces to each other. Emma's tutor was astounded at how much Emma wrote, but I was not surprised. Emma had all the basic skills she needed for drafting and the most important thing to do was to stay out of her way and give her time to write.

Often children and tutors become overly reliant on each other. It is important that we do not let tutoring stifle the child. When we work with children who are struggling, we get accustomed to giving help and they get accustomed to receiving it. We always must keep in mind that the objective is independence and get out of the way when the child can operate alone.

Minilessons

think aloud

Minilessons for transition readers depend on what the child knows and needs to know. To follow up the lesson with Trevor who was learning to retell a story in his own words, I might have taught a minilesson on *think-aloud.* Think-aloud explains what you are thinking as you are reading. By saying his or her thoughts out loud, the tutor makes it possible for children to hear the processes of a skilled reader, which are normally not observable.

In this minilesson, I would explain that it is important for readers to think about what they read and that saying it in your head is one way to ensure understanding.

Figure 3
Emma's Bubble Chart

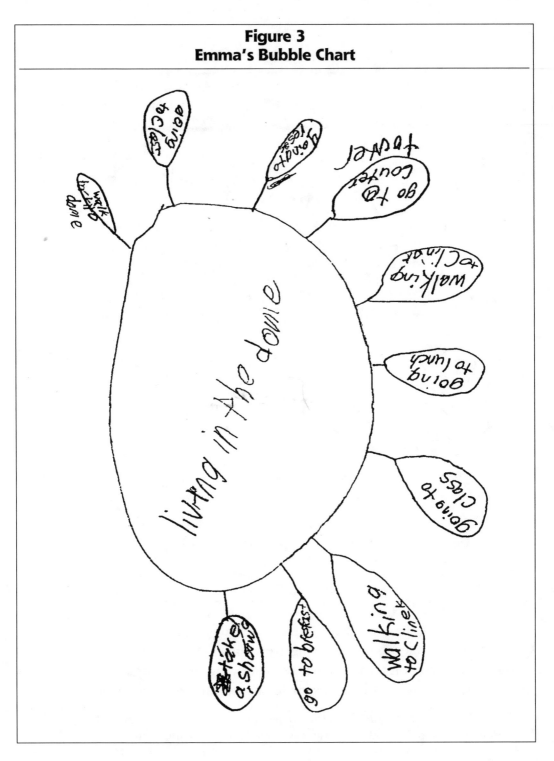

Figure 4
Dr. Roller's Bubble Chart

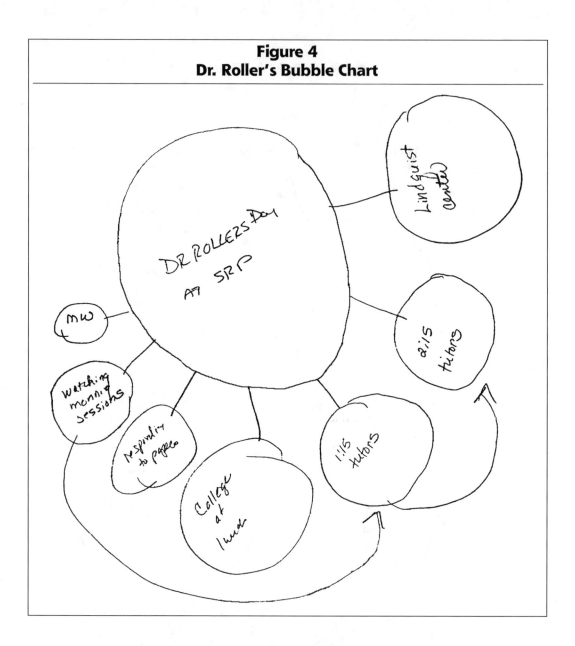

Children often think this means saying everything that happened on the page (just as Trevor did). What it means, however, is deciding the important things and saying them in one's own words. For example, suppose the page said the following:

> I tell Mom and Dad, "There are two beavers at the dock!" "Beavers eat bark," Dad says. Mom says, "And they build with sticks and branches. They must be building a lodge."

Some children might think I wanted them to tell me exactly what happened, just as Trevor did when we were reading *Beavers Beware!* However, the point is for the child to think about the important ideas in his or her own words. The tutor might then model as I did for Trevor.

Figure 5
Activities for Transition Readers

Reading Easy Books
1. Child chooses book.
2. Child reads book.
3. Child and tutor talk about book either before, during, or after reading.

Reading the New Book
1. Child chooses book from tutor's selection.
2. Book Introduction
   a. Read title.
   b. Look at cover and predict what it is about.
   c. Read back cover or cover flap.
3. Child reads the book silently stopping at intervals to discuss meaning and difficulties.

Writing
1. Child decides what he or she wants to write.
2. Child writes draft using temporary spelling.
3. Child and tutor edit the writing.
4. Child writes (or tutor may type) final copy.

Minilesson
1. Tutor introduces the lesson which is based on recent performance of the child.
2. Tutor models and explains.
3. Tutor asks for feedback.
4. Tutor follows up on lesson in actual reading.

Reading Challenging Books
1. Child chooses book.
2. Tutor and child read the book together using a comfortable pattern of taking turns. Focus is on enjoying the book and instruction is kept to a minimum.

Sometimes children have a hard time learning to summarize and go beyond the text instead of just repeating every detail verbatim. Alternating turns with the child after each page or paragraph often helps, because the child has the benefit of a good model and coaching while he or she tries to understand what to do. When the tutor feels the child understands, the child can take over and the tutor can assist as necessary.

This kind of lesson is particularly important for children who have had trouble learning to read. Because they usually have trouble learning how to pronounce the words, their early instruction often emphasizes saying the words, and many struggling readers have a very word-oriented concept of reading. They think reading is saying the words right and they often do not really think about what the words mean.

Reading Challenging Books

For the transition reader, reading challenging books is usually a matter of having someone (or sometimes a machine) nearby to help with important unknown words. Paired reading as defined on page 15 usually is not necessary. One way to motivate challenging reading is to have children develop a presentation or a report about a topic they have chosen. Sometimes this can be done in group settings and it is not necessary in tutoring sessions. But sometimes a child will be so interested in the project that she will ask to have particular books and parts of books read aloud to her. Recording books on tape is another way to approach the challenging reading activity for transition readers. You may also want to read the section titled "Making Difficult Books Accessible" in *Variability Not Disability*, Chapter 4. An overview of the tutoring session for transition readers is provided in Figure 5.

FOR THE SUPERVISOR

Tutors may find the amount of information in this chapter overwhelming. Reassure them that they are not expected to know, understand, and remember everything. Explain that the chapter is intended to give a broad overview of tutoring. Suggest that they read the chapter quickly realizing that they may want to pay more attention to the sections that pertain to the level of child they are tutoring and referring to Figure 1, 2, or 5 (depending on their child's level) to help them remember the activities. They also may want to return to Chapter 1 after they have tutored their child several times.

Chapter 2

Understanding the Complexity of Reading

MOST PEOPLE *who decide to be reading tutors are fairly skilled readers.* Because they are so skilled, it is sometimes hard for them to understand why learning to read is so difficult for some children. Although reading is second nature to skilled readers, it only became second nature after much learning and practice. Reading is very complex, and that is why it is so difficult for some children to learn.

This chapter explains how skilled readers read. This is rather presumptuous because there are still many aspects of skilled reading that researchers and educators do not completely understand. However, I will share what we do understand. I want to caution that an understanding of *skilled* reading does not equal an understanding of reading tutoring. Beginners and experts often do things differently and learners pass through stages as they acquire the information that skilled readers use easily and often without conscious attention. Yet it is important to understand what skilled readers do; understanding the goal we are traveling toward helps in the journey.

KNOWLEDGE AND PROCESSES

Figure 6 is a simplified representation of recent conceptions of skilled reading. The three large boxes—Box A labeled Lower Level Processes, Box B labeled Working Memory, and Box C labeled Higher Level Processes—contain information used by readers. The reader takes information from the text (at the top left of the diagram) into Box A where decoding and vocabulary information (sometimes influenced through working memory by the remaining four information types) is used to retrieve pronunciations and meanings. These are placed in Working Memory where they combine with information from the higher level processes (grammar, cohesion, passage structure, and world knowledge) to process the text and hopefully arrive at meaning.

Before discussing the ways that readers use information sources, it is important to understand the kinds of processes and information that each box represents. Lack of information in any part of the model can cause reading difficulties. Perhaps the best way to understand what each type of information contributes to reading is to experience difficulty with that type of information.

The symbol that follows presents a problem: ǫnibopəb (see Box 1, Decoding). In this case you cannot translate the visual symbols into anything you recognize because the symbols have been reversed as they would be in a mirror. Most skilled readers, however, eventually are able to figure out what the symbols represent. There are probably several ways to do so. One is to realize that the letters are backward and to identify the first three symbols as -ing. Then the bs may be identified as ds and, given access to the /d/ sound and the context of this paragraph, the word is identified as decoding. Although this is not the process skilled readers use during ordinary reading, it does demonstrate several sources of information available to them. For example the recognition of common word elements such as -ing, the availability of sound-letter information such as the /d/ sound that goes with the letter d, and the contextual information available from the surrounding text. The type of information used by skilled readers in ordinary reading is the subject of much controversy and will be discussed in the following section.

Vocabulary (Box 2) is illustrated by this excerpt from Lewis Carroll's "Jabberwocky" (1973):

> 'Twas brillig and the slithy toves
> Did gyre and gimble in the wabe.
> All mimsy were the borogoves,
> And the momes rath outgrabe.

The poem's meaning seems almost within grasp, but we do not have meanings for words like *brillig*, *slithy*, *toves*, and the other content words of the poem, and ultimately we cannot make sense of it. Readers face vocabulary problems when they lack meaning for the words in a text. Although "Jabberwocky" is a contrived example, real

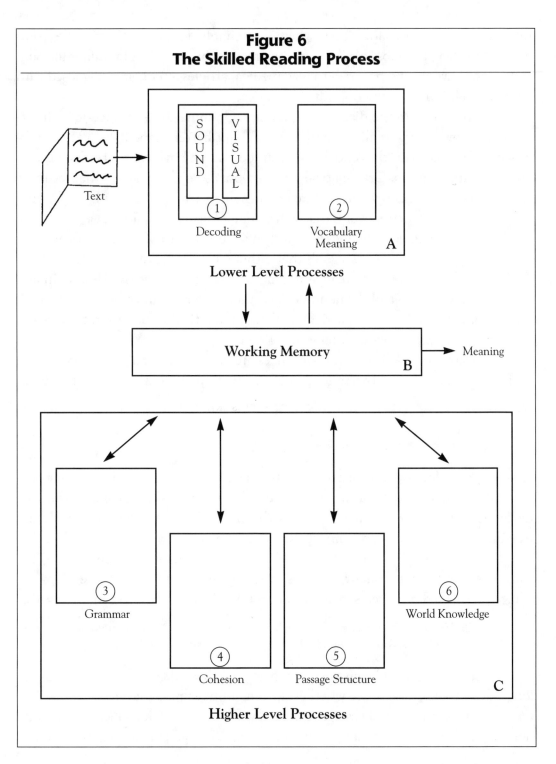

Figure 6
The Skilled Reading Process

Text

S O U N D | V I S U A L

① ②

Decoding | Vocabulary Meaning

A

Lower Level Processes

Working Memory B → Meaning

③ Grammar

④ Cohesion

⑤ Passage Structure

⑥ World Knowledge

C

Higher Level Processes

readers sometimes encounter texts where they simply do not know what the words mean. This happens most often when they read technical prose in unfamiliar subject areas. Anyone who has tried to read medical articles after being diagnosed with an unfamiliar illness knows this difficulty.

The third box in the diagram is grammar. Grammar (or sentence-level information) allows you to realize that you are in a lot better shape if "you ate the dinosaur" than you are if "the dinosaur ate you" because in English, word order conveys important information. Grammatical information also makes you feel that meaning is just beyond your grasp when you are reading "Jabberwocky." Because the familiar English words are function words that signal grammatical information, we expect the unfamiliar words to actually mean something. Consider the first line: *'Twas brillig and the slithy toves*. The *'Twas* signals that either a noun or an adjective will follow. The words *the slithy toves* are read as a noun phrase because *the* signals a noun and the *es* in *toves* suggests a plural noun. *Slithy* is then read as a kind of a tove, or an adjective. Skilled readers assign a great deal of grammatical information to words in sentences as they go about making sense of them.

Cohesion (Box 4) is the way sentences are connected. You should have some difficulty connecting the two sentences of this text taken from Halliday and Hasan (1976):

> Time flies.
> You can't; they fly too quickly.

However, once I reveal that *time* is the verb and *flies* is the noun and that the first sentence is asking you to use a timing device to measure flies' flight speed, the sentences should make sense. Now you know that *Time flies* is what you cannot do, and that *they* is the *flies*. You can connect the two sentences.

It is a bit more difficult to demonstrate a passage structure problem (Box 5) because passage structure usually operates over large segments of text. The following paragraph adapted from Pearson and Johnson (1978) should give you an impression:

> Birds build nests in many places. Eagles build nests on cliffs. Robins build nests in trees. Pheasants build nests on the ground. Pheasants have beautiful feathers.

The last sentence probably jars you, and most readers would say that it does not belong. They would pause to see whether they might have read the wrong words. The sentence breaks the rules of passage structure, where a general main idea, "Birds build nests in many places," is followed by specific supporting details—eagles and cliffs, robins and trees, and pheasants and the ground. The violation forces you to check your comprehension. Skilled readers are familiar with many types of passage structures—narratives or stories that follow time order and usually include setting, character, problems, events, solutions, and resolutions; or expository (informational) texts that use general to specific, cause and effect, and problem and solution organizations. They also are familiar with devices that signal passage structure such as headings, outlines, and introductory paragraphs.

Perhaps one of the most critical factors determining comprehension is the relation between what the reader already knows about a topic and what is on the page. The paragraph that follows gives you the experience of reading something for which readers do not have appropriate background knowledge:

> If the balloons popped, the sound wouldn't be able to carry because everything would be too far away from the correct floor. A closed window would also prevent the sound from carrying, because most buildings tend to be well insulated. Because the whole operation depends on the steady flow of electricity, a break in the middle of the wire would also cause problems. Of course, the fellow could shout, but the human voice is not loud enough to carry that far. An additional problem is that a string could break on the instrument. Then there would be no accompaniment to the message. It is clear that the best situation would involve less distance. Then there would be fewer potential problems. With face-to-face contact, the least number of things could go wrong (Bransford & Johnson, 1972).

Readers who are asked to rewrite this passage in their own words after reading it have a difficult time. They can decode and assign meanings to the words and they can organize the sentences and connect them. They even understand that this is an expository structure that is cataloging possible problems. What they lack is knowledge about the situation.

However, after looking at the picture in Figure 7, it is much easier to remember the passage. The picture provides important information that helps you attach incoming information from the text to your prior world knowledge. Without it there is too wide a gap between the new (the passage) and the known (the picture) and comprehension fails.

How Are the Information Sources Used?

Although there is reasonable agreement among psychologists and educators on the kinds of information available to skilled readers during reading, there is less agreement about how this information is used and which types of information are

Figure 7
Modern-Day Romeo

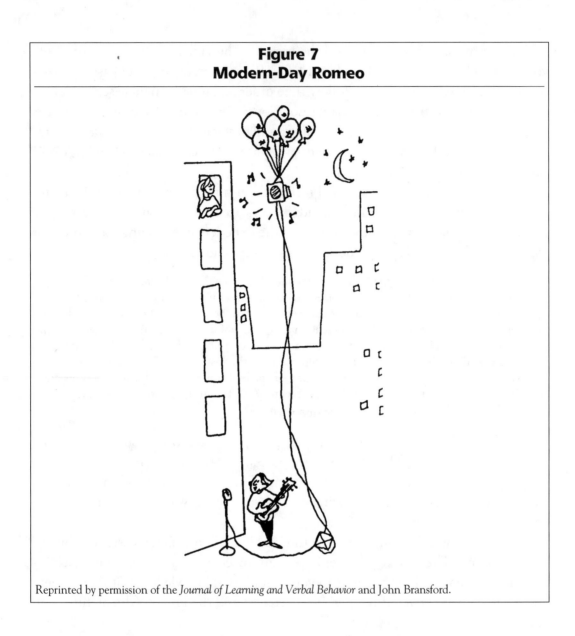

Reprinted by permission of the *Journal of Learning and Verbal Behavior* and John Bransford.

most important. Most of the arguments center around whether it is lower level information and processes (decoding and accessing word meaning) or higher level processes (the remaining boxes of our representation in Figure 6) that make the difference between good readers and poor readers. Those who take different positions have disagreements about whether sound information, visual information, or contextual information is most important in skilled reading. The answer is that both higher and lower level processes can cause reading problems. The argument is really about which information causes the most problems for the most people.

Psychologists' arguments about how the information sources are used are important because they often are used to support particular approaches to reading instruction—particularly beginning reading instruction. The most important question for tutoring is "How should we begin reading instruction?" Some experts argue that we should begin at the level of individual letters because skilled readers use letter sounds (sound information in Box 1) to identify words. Others argue that we should begin at the whole-word level because skilled readers pay a great deal of attention to words (visual information in Box 1) and do not pay much attention to letter sounds. Still other experts argue that we should begin at the story level because skilled readers rely on contextual meaning (information from boxes 3 to 6) to figure out words and do not pay much attention to individual words. Because these questions are ultimately very important, I will explain the psychological arguments in the following sections, but first I will define some words used in these arguments.

There are several kinds of information that help readers recognize words: sound-code information, visual-code information, and contextual information. For the purposes of this discussion I will relate these three terms to Figure 6: (1) sound-code information in Box 1, (2) visual-code information in Box 1, and (3) contextual information in Boxes 3 through 6. Using sound-code information to identify words means that the sounds of letters or letter groups (such as /c/ /a/ /t/) are blended together to identify the word *cat*. Using visual codes means matching the features of the letters on the page to stored visual images of the word and identifying it without using the letter sounds. Contextual information aids word identification by limiting the possibilities. For example, in the sentence, "As she stepped out of the house after the last spring snow melted away, she was dazzled by the brilliant green of the _____" we can predict almost certainly that the missing word is *grass*.

Visual Codes or Sound Codes

The important argument over whether children should first be taught sound codes or whole words (visual codes) is related to the psychological controversy over whether skilled readers identify words using the sound code or whether they directly match visual features of the word on the page to a stored visual image of the word (the visual code). Like most either-or arguments, the answer is that skilled readers can and do use both. The issue is which code predominates under what circumstances.

29

Again a caution is necessary. Psychologists for the most part agree that skilled readers use sound representations for words at some point in the reading process. They disagree about when readers use the sound code. Do they use it to *identify* the word, or do they identify the word using the *visual code* and *then* assign a sound code in order to remember it? The question is when the sound code is used and why.

One likely resolution to this argument suggests that readers may initially identify unfamiliar words using the sound code, but that as the word is encountered repeatedly a unified visual image is formed and the word can be identified more quickly through the visual code than it can through the sound code. This explanation is consistent with psychological evidence. For example, frequently occurring words are identified more quickly than infrequently occurring words, suggesting that repeated encounters may result in a stored image that provides quicker identification. In addition, words that are consistent with English spelling rules are identified more quickly than those that are inconsistent, suggesting that familiar patterns are consolidated into identifiable images.

Another source of evidence, this one pointing to the use of the sound code, is the reading of "pseudowords" and "real" words by skilled and less-skilled readers. A pseudoword is a fake word: It follows the rules of English spelling but it is not actually an English word. The words in "Jabberwocky" like *gyre*, *gimble*, and *wabe* are examples of pseudowords. Skilled readers read pseudowords much more quickly than less-skilled readers. Because these words have not been read before, the skilled readers cannot be faster because they have developed a direct visual code for the word; they are simply better at using the sound code. For unfamiliar words the differences between skilled and less-skilled readers are similar to those for pseudowords. However, for familiar words that both skilled and less-skilled readers have encountered many times there is much less difference in the amount of time they take to identify the word. The large differences with pseudowords and unfamiliar words and the much smaller differences with familiar words suggest that the repeated encounters result in the creation of visual image that allows faster identification.

Early in the history of this debate, some psychologists thought that skilled readers always used the sound code to identify a word and argued that because skilled readers used the sound code it was important to focus on the sound code with beginning readers. Now that we know skilled readers often use the visual code to identify words, one might argue that early instruction should focus on visual codes and whole-word recognition. Once again we may be making a false interpretation of what we should teach beginning readers based on what skilled readers do. It may be that skilled readers become skilled because they use the sound code very efficiently. This allows them to read unfamiliar words that upon repeated encounters acquire a strong visual representation.

It seems sensible that because skilled readers use both sound and visual codes, we must teach both, and the question of which should be taught first or whether they should be taught together cannot be answered on the basis of skilled reading. We must continually keep in mind that skilled reading develops over time. Expert readers may be able to read in particular ways only because they have gradually developed their ways of reading. Beginners may not be able to read in the ways that experts do because they do not have the knowledge that experts have amassed over many hours of reading. Ultimately reading instruction must be consistent with the possibilities suggested by skilled reading, but understanding skilled reading is only part of the information we need to make decisions about instruction.

Predictability and the Use of Context

Another major argument concerns whether skilled readers use context to predict upcoming words. This argument is important for tutoring because its supporters argue that we should begin reading instruction at the story level because context is so important in identifying words. The research literature shows quite clearly that skilled readers do use prediction to help them with comprehension processes (Stanovich, 1991). At issue is whether skilled readers use prediction to help them recognize words. We know skilled readers can predict words—as shown in the example of predicting the word *grass* earlier—but do skilled readers predict words in normal ongoing reading?

At one end of the spectrum are top-down arguments (arguments that contend reading moves from the reader's head down to the print) that say skilled readers do predict words and simply sample print to confirm their predictions. At the other end of the spectrum are bottom-up arguments (arguments that contend reading moves from the print up to the reader's head) that assert skilled readers do not predict words because their sound and visual information processors analyze print so completely and efficiently that they do not need to predict words. In the middle are arguments suggesting that information from both top-down and bottom-up sources interact during word recognition.

The extreme positions described in the preceding paragraph are untenable. You cannot read without print. On the other hand it is true that skilled readers read sentences and paragraphs faster than they read lists of unrelated words; context does facilitate word reading to some degree (Crowder & Wagner, 1992). The question becomes which information sources have the most influence—higher level or lower level.

The research evidence is relatively clear that for skilled readers bottom-up processes are heavily involved in word recognition. One source of evidence comes from eye-movement studies. In these studies readers read text from a computer screen while the computer keeps track of where the eye moves. To gain a better understanding of these studies, take a magazine and poke a small hole in the middle of a page that has a lot of print. Recruit a friend or family member to read the page. As they read the page, look through the small hole and focus on one of their eyes. The eye will "jerk" along from left to right and then sweep back to the left and begin to jerk along again. Occasionally the eye may move backward. The jerky motion is produced by the alternation of "saccades" (movements) and "fixations" (stops). The sweep, which is the movement of the eye from the end of the line to the beginning of the next, is called a "return sweep"; occasionally the eye stops in the middle of the line and goes back. This is called a regression. Computer data show that on the average, readers fixate or stop every 1.33 words (Crowder & Wagner, 1972). The eyes stop on almost all content words and only occasionally skip small words like *a*, *and*, and *the*. It simply is not true that readers predict words and only sample the print to confirm predictions. They actually look at and process most words.

Another kind of evidence that often is used to prove that skilled readers do not use bottom-up information is the fact that readers can and often do read text with typographical errors without noticing them. Gough (1995) has presented evidence that although readers do not consciously notice the errors, they do affect readers' speed if you have sensitive enough measurement devices (devices that can record milliseconds.) Therefore, evidence about errors cannot be used to argue that we should rely on context and whole stories at the beginning of reading instruction.

Another problem with the notion that skilled readers predict words is that words in natural text are not very predictable. Many of the experiments that were used to show that context aids word recognition used very predictable sentences like the one about grass that I used earlier where the probability that the reader will say "grass" is very high. However, studies of a variety of types of ordinary texts show that the probability of predicting a particular word is usually between 20% and 35%. Furthermore, the words that are most predictable are the little words like *a*, *an*, and *the* that do not carry a lot of information.

The argument that children's reading instruction should not focus on bottom-up processes because skilled readers do not use them is faulty because it is not true that skilled readers do not use these processes. They focus on nearly all the words and they use the sound and visual codes so quickly that they do not need to predict words. They can save their predictions to deal with higher order comprehension work. So the argument that we should focus on whole stories and that we do not need to teach sounds and letters in words is wrong.

The evidence indicates that sounds, letters, and words are important, and that children need to learn all of them. However, nothing in the data on skilled readers tells us the order in which these elements should be taught.

Social Context and Motivation

What the discussion in previous sections lacks is any attention to the motivation to read. That the skilled reader wants to read is taken for granted. This is not the case however, for many children and adults, particularly those who think they do not read well. Let me quote a student who turned to me as we were videotaping a reading lesson and said:

> If I tell you something, I'm not going to hurt your feelings? Because I can't read very good. And see, I want to read very good. And I can't. So I don't like it very much.

We know that skilled readers are motivated to read, but we have not studied how they become motivated until recently. Interest in the Soviet psychologists Vygotsky and Bahktin has called to our attention the importance of context (surrounding social conditions) in the reading process. Skilled readers have learned to read in settings that emphasize the importance, benefits, and enjoyment of reading. Because they value reading and because they are good at it the motivation to read is strong and lasts a lifetime.

The importance of valuing reading is one of the reasons it is so important to place phonics instruction in the context of a total reading–language arts program. If reading is seen as only sounding out words, there is not much point to it. I have seen many children who have learned to sound out words yet have no desire so to do. They can read but do not want to. Instruction that assumes motivation is likely to fail with many children. Motivation must be an important consideration in reading instruction, which is a strong argument for using whole, interesting books. Again the evidence does not allow us to argue about the order of stories, words, sounds, and letters, but it is clear that all are important.

WHAT DOES RESEARCH ABOUT SKILLED READING TELL US ABOUT BEGINNING READING INSTRUCTION?

After reading the section "How Are the Information Sources Used?" you may be asking, What *can* we conclude from skilled reading about beginning reading instruction? I have made the point that we must be very cautious when using accounts of skilled reading to decide about beginning reading instruction. The argument that we should not focus on the sound code in beginning reading because skilled readers do not use the code very much in reading is clearly an error. However that does not mean that the counterargument, that we should focus on the sound code first and primarily because skilled readers do use the sound code sometimes, is correct. Skilled readers use many sources of information in reading and we cannot generalize about their skilled use and thereby make assumptions about beginning reading.

What does seem clear is that children need to learn many different kinds of information. What seems sensible, although we still lack a clear answer, is to try to teach the sound code in the context of a balanced reading program that keeps sight of the overall purpose of reading: to get meaning. This program should also make sure that children have mastered the sound code and built a good sight vocabulary through the visual code. The International Reading Association (IRA) has developed a position statement on the teaching of the sound code—phonics. It is a good representation of what skilled reading professionals conclude based on what is known from psychology and the practice of teaching reading. "The Role of Phonics in Reading Instruction" (1997) sets forth three basic assertions regarding phonics and the teaching of reading:

1. The teaching of phonics is an important aspect of beginning reading instruction.
2. Classroom teachers in the primary grades do value and do teach phonics as a part of their reading programs.
3. Phonics instruction, to be effective in promoting independence in reading, must be embedded in the context of a total reading/language arts program.

Notice that IRA agrees phonics is important and that it is only part of what must be taught in beginning reading.

FOR THE SUPERVISOR

After reading the "Knowledge and Processes" section of this chapter, your tutors understand what kinds of information are important to readers and what happens when each kind of information is disrupted. You may want to do a further demonstration of how automatic the decoding processes of skilled readers are. Try the Stroop task (Stroop, 1935): Use a set of colored pencils to write two 20-word columns of color words. In both columns, use four or five different colors. In the first column write the color of each pencil. Use the blue pencil to write *blue* and the green pencil to write *green*. In the second column write the exact same words, but always use a pencil of a different color to write each color word. For example, use a blue pencil to write *green* and the green pencil to write *red*. Then time yourself as you tell the color of the ink for each word in the column. For example, in the first column where you have written the word *blue* in blue ink you would say "blue," and for the word *green*, written in green ink, you would say "green." In the second column where *blue* is written in green ink, you would say "green" as a response to *blue* because you are telling the color of the ink. To the word *red* you respond "green" because it is written in green ink. You will find is that it is very difficult to say "green" when you are looking at the word *red* written in green ink. That is because your decoding skills are so second nature that when you see the word *blue* you cannot help thinking blue, even though you are trying to focus on the green color of the ink. Skilled readers decode so well that they can hardly keep themselves from reading when words are in front of them.

Your tutors may be confused by the "How Are the Information Sources Used?" section. There has been a lot of media coverage of the debates on teaching beginning reading and the arguments are complex. Few tutors will have escaped the phonics versus whole language media debacle, and they will be concerned about "doing the right thing." The position I take here is that both types of instruction are important and should be included in balanced reading instruction and that there are simply no definitive answers to the question of how to teach beginning reading. The answer to how to teach beginning reading has been elusive—probably because there is so much variability in the ways that individual children learn best. This variability is a strong argument for individual tutoring. Tutors are in a position to provide each child with whatever that child happens to need. The tutors will need assurance that you will help them make wise decisions about what to teach their child.

Chapter 3

Reading and Writing Development

GOOD ONE-ON-ONE *tutoring is effective partly because the tutor can judge what the child knows and can do.* The tutor then can help the child learn what he or she needs to learn next. Tutors can only do this if they know what reading and writing behavior look like and understand how behaviors follow one another. This chapter outlines typical reading and writing development so that you will recognize the various phases of development and be able to place a child's behaviors appropriately. Understanding development will help you make good decisions about what comes next for the child you are tutoring.

One important caution is in order here: All children do not develop in exactly the same way. The advantage of one-on-one tutoring is that each child's unique development can be accommodated. Although this chapter talks about typical patterns of development, you may find that the children you work with do not fit the typical pattern. Instead of trying to make the child fit the pattern, ask, "What can this child do? Why is it that this child can do this but not that? What is the most important information or strategy to learn next?"

In both reading and writing children seem to follow a general sequence. Elizabeth Sulzby (as cited in Morrow, 1997) has described developmental trends for young children's reading and writing behavior, which are presented in Table 1. Remember, the fact that she has listed phases does not mean that all children pass through each phase discretely and in order. Some children may exhibit features of several phases simultaneously and some may skip particular phases.

WRITING DEVELOPMENT

Very young children do not distinguish between writing and drawing. When asked to write something they will draw a picture (see Table 1, Phase 1 of Writing Development). If asked to read their "writing," they may tell you a story to go with the picture or point to parts of the drawing and name them. However, gradually children understand that adult writing is different than drawing. At this point, they begin to scribble (Phase 2). Again when asked to read they tell a story as they look at their scribbles. An interesting feature of scribble writing is that although it does not include actual letters, it usually resembles the writing system used in the child's en-

---

Table 1
Sulzby's Descriptions of Early Reading and Writing Development

Writing Development

Phase 1	use of drawings for writing	
Phase 2	scribble writing	
Phase 3	use of letter-like forms	
Phase 4	use of well-learned units or letter strings	
Phase 5	use of invented spelling	
Phase 6	writing conventionally	

Development of Storybook Reading

Phase 1	attending to pictures but not forming stories	
Phase 2	attending to pictures and forming oral stories	
Phase 3	attending to a mix of pictures, reading, and storytelling	
Phase 4	attending to print but forming stories	
Phase 5	attending to print but occasionally reverting to pictures and storytelling	
Phase 6	reading conventionally	

Cited in Morrow, L.M. (1997). *Literacy Development With Early Teachers* (pp. 141 and 198). Needham Heights, MA: Allyn & Bacon.

---

vironment. For example, scribble writing for children writing in English consists mostly of loops and connecting lines like those in Figure 8. However, children whose writing system includes a lot of dots and apostrophes and accent marks will include dots and slashes above the line of writing, and children from Hebrew and Arabic backgrounds have scribbles that resemble Hebrew and Arabic scripts.

Gradually the children's scribbles begin to look more like actual letters. Children in English-language settings begin to produce forms that contain the actual elements of the English alphabet (Phase 3). The forms are composed of circles and curves, and horizontal, vertical, and diagonal lines. In the next phase (Phase 4) children actually have learned to spell some familiar words such as their own name, family members' names, *Mom*, *Dad*, *love*, *the*, *is*, and *dog*. These conventional spellings (which may be out of order or have the letters turned around) are combined with random strings of letters to create stories.

Most children selected for reading tutoring will be in the last two of Sulzby's phases, invented spelling and conventional spelling; usually they will be in transition between them. Invented spellings are the spellings that children create to represent words before they actually know how to spell them. For example, a child might write *HOSPDL* to represent hospital. Several researchers have studied children's invented spelling and found that it develops gradually and eventually gives way to conventional spelling (Read, 1986; Sowers, 1984).

Spelling Development

Susan Sowers (1984) suggests that there are two major lines of development for invented spelling: a progression for the position of letters represented (random strings, beginning sounds, and beginning and ending sounds); and changes in the information source the child uses for spelling (mouth, ears, eyes, and knowledge). In other words children write letter strings first. Then they begin to put the beginning letters of words in their writing. After they are using the correct beginning letters for many words, they begin to get the ending letter correct as well, and finally they begin to fill in the middles correctly. When they first begin to write they often use the sounds at the beginning of letter names to represent a sound. For example, a child might say *d* and realize that his or her mouth was in the same position as when saying *Dad*. You can actually see the child experimenting with exaggerated mouth movements alternating between *d* and *Dad*. Soon the child will be able to hear the

Figure 8
Scribble Writing

similarities in sounds without attention to mouth position. Finally the child will begin to remember how the word looks and will then begin to spell conventionally.

In the early stages of invented spelling children may use a single letter to stand for each word. Usually this is the first letter of the word. For example, in Figure 9 the child drew a picture and wrote, *i c m*, to represent, *I climbed mountains.* Gradually the child uses more letters.

Figure 10 (on pages 42–43) shows a child using mostly single letters and also the conventional spelling for *is* and *SMR* to represent summer. As noted earlier, in the early stages the child often uses articulation (positions of the mouth and tongue) to determine spellings. For example, the child may spell *when* with a y (*yen*) because the sound at the beginning of *when* is made the same way as the sound at the beginning of the letter name y. One child represented *chicken* as *HKN*—probably because the sound at the end of the letter name *H* is the same as the sound that begins *chicken*. Children's early use of short vowel sounds is related closely to articulation. For example, the short sound of /e/ as in *bet* often is spelled with an *a* because the articulation of the letter name *a* begins with a sound that is very similar to the /e/ sound. Similarly short /i/ as in *fit* is closer to the letter name *e* than to *i*, so children often

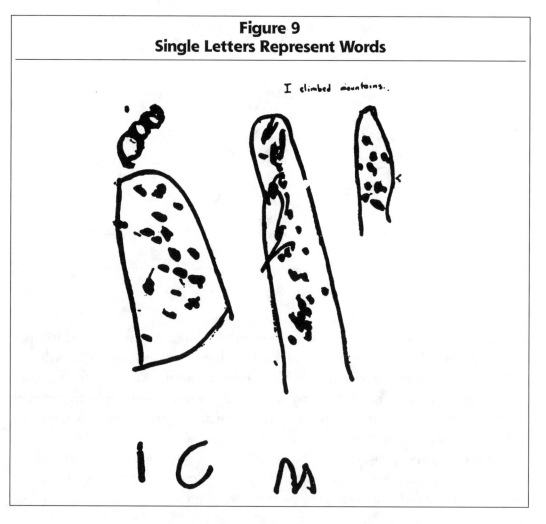

Figure 9
Single Letters Represent Words

I climbed mountains..

represent the short /i/ sound with an *e*. Gradually however children move away from articulation and use sounds heard. As their exposure to print grows they gradually rely more on memory of what they have seen and finally learn to use the conventional spellings of words they have learned.

Figure 11 (on page 44) is the writing of an older child who had difficulty developing conventional spelling. Within this one sample there are examples of several phrases operating in the same piece of writing. The child used conventional spellings for many words including *a, the, went, she, then, I*, and *for*. There may be a trace of some of the articulation strategies for short vowel sounds as for example in writing *viset* for *visit*—the second *i* in *visit* sounds a lot more like the letter name *e* than it does *i*, and perhaps in *want* for *went* in the second boxed paragraph. There are many places where it is apparent that the child is relying on sound: *hospdl, wok* and *woking* for *walk* and *walking, opurashun, crdligis*, and *kruchis*. The child consistently used *u* to represent the /u/ sound in *wus, becuss*, and *Grandmu*. There are also places where the child seems to rely on a combination of sound and visual information. For example, the use of the *a* in *therapy* suggests some visual memory of the word as does *won* for *one* where the short *u* sound is not represented with *u* as it is in *wus, becus*, and *Grandmu. Wus ant* may indicate some visual memory for the *a* in *wasn't*. This last example should emphasize clearly the earlier point that these phases are not necessarily sequential and separate.

Content Development

To this point the discussion has centered on writing development as it relates to the spelling system. However, the content of children's writing also develops over time. They begin with the simple labeling of pictures and gradually they learn to incorporate the elements of setting, characters, plots, and themes to create stories. Many young children's first stories are *bed to bed* stories, simple listings of all the things they did in a day: "I got up. I ate breakfast. I brushed my teeth..." until once again they are bedded down for the night. Characters in early stories are almost always friends and family members or familiar fictional characters from cartoons, movies, and children's books. When children begin to invent characters you may find that the characters behave erratically from episode to episode and that children only gradually develop the concept of character as a consistent individual with understandable psychological motivations.

Figure 10
Mixed Conventional and Phonetic Spellings

FEB 9:1992

I M G A B D
I am getting a bike for

S M R
summer.

A E IS I
It is a

loONAD
100 dollars.

continued

Children's plots also develop over time. Plots in early writing are almost lists of unconnected events; they gradually take the form of problems with multiple episodes or attempts at resolution that eventually resolve. Ultimately the child's repertoire expands to include other forms of writing such as poetry, persuasion, logical arguments, and essays.

Figure 10
Mixed Conventional and Phonetical Spellings (continued)

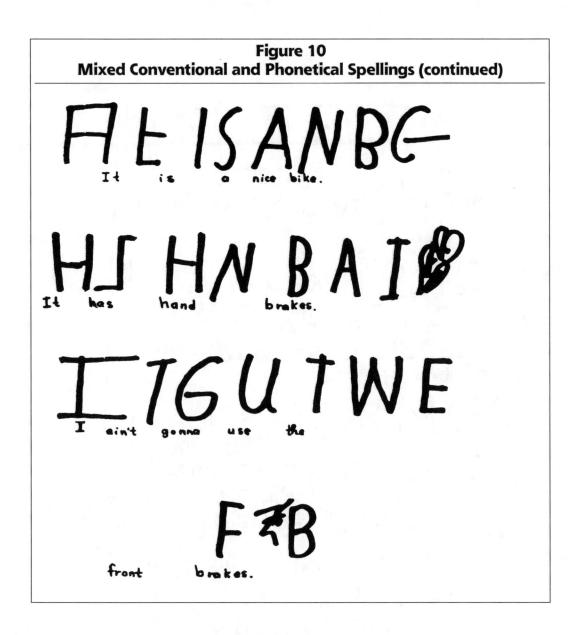

READING DEVELOPMENT

Table 1 also lists Sulzby's phases of reading development. Sulzby identified these stages by presenting children ages 2 through 5 with a storybook and asking them to read it to her. The stages she lists are descriptions of what various children did at various ages. Once again these are not step-by-step phases that are always clearly

Figure 11
Multiple Phases in One Sample

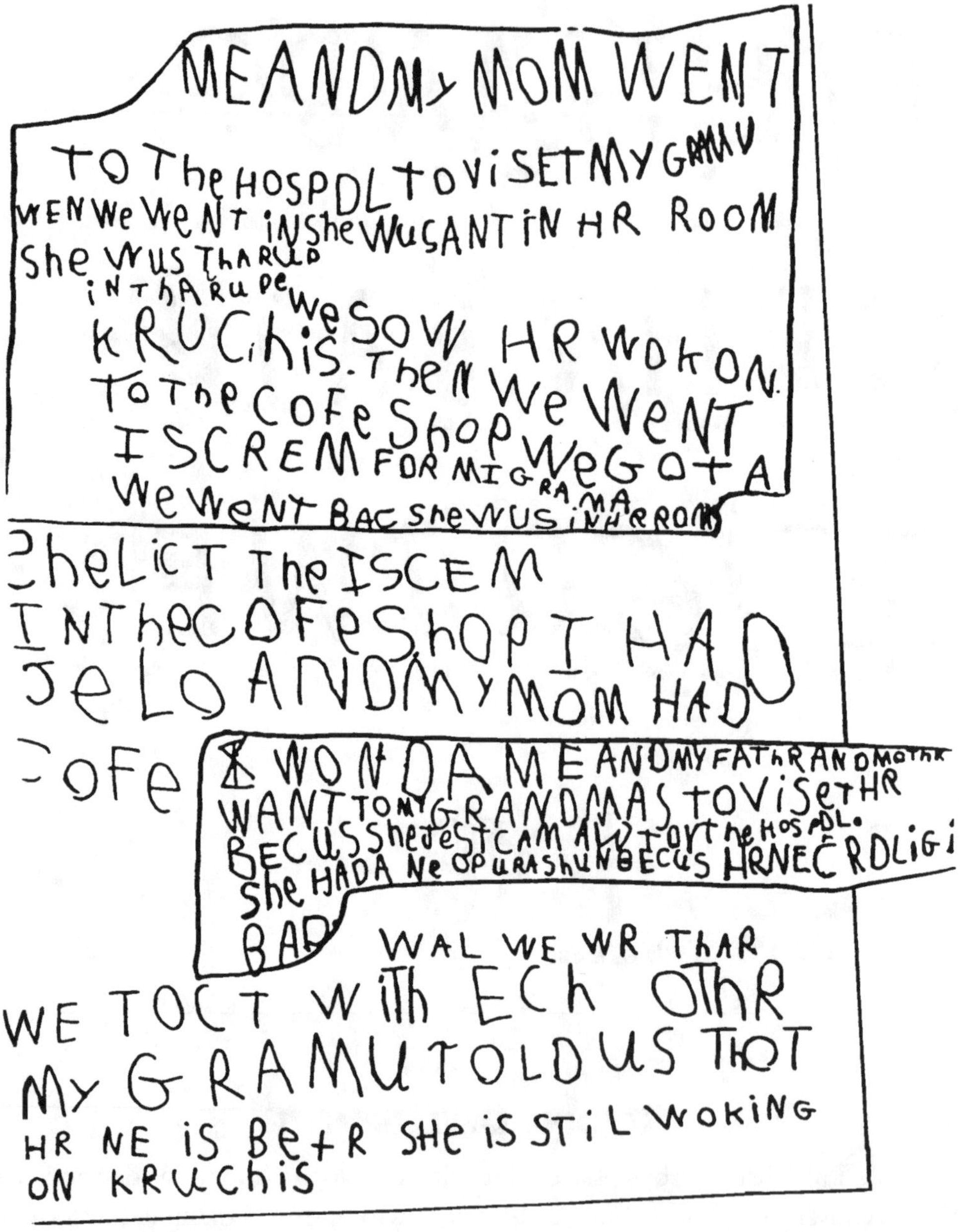

ME AND My MOM WENT
TO The HOSPDL TO ViSET MY GRAMU
WEN We WeNT iN She WUS ANT iN HR ROOM
She WUS ThA RUD
iN ThA RU DE
KRUCihiS. We SOW HR WOK ON.
ToThe COFe Shop Then We WeNT
I SCREM FOR Mi GRA MA We GOT A
We WeNT BAC She WUS iN HR ROOM

She LiCT The ISCEM
IN The COFe Shop T HAD
Je LO AND My MOM HAD
COFe I WONDA ME AND My FATHR AND MOThR
WANT To My GRANDMAS To ViSeT HR
BECUS She JeST CAM AL 2 OUT The HOSPDL.
She HAD A Ne OPURAShUN BECUS HR NE C RD LiGi
BAD WAL WE WR ThAR
WE TOCT WiTH ECh OThR
My GRAMU TOLD US ThOT
HR NE iS BE+R SHE iS STiL WOKiNG
ON KRUChiS

distinguishable and that all children pass through in sequential order. Much of what a child does at a particular age is dependent on his or her own particular experiences with storybook reading. However, on average, children seem to progress through these various phases.

Learning to Read Storybooks

In Phase 1, the child reads by turning the pages and talking about what is on them. He or she may point to an illustration and identify it or tell something else about the picture. A child in this phase does not necessarily follow the story line of the book or connect the pictures from page to page and build a story. This happens in Phase 2, in which the child uses the pictures to help in telling a story. The story he or she tells does not sound like a "book" story but rather like stories that we tell each other in casual talk. Often to understand the story you must be looking at the pictures with the child.

In the next phase the child continues to "read" the pictures, but the talk that accompanies the pictures begins to change. There is a transition between oral story telling and talk that sounds like the reading of a book or literary language. For example, in this phase the child may begin with, "Once upon a time," and include information about setting, characters, plot, and theme in her story. The child's story alternates between oral-story language and literary-story language. In Phase 4 the child looks at the pictures but tells a literary story. The child sounds like he or she is "reading" in both wording and intonation. If you were not watching the book you would think the child was reading; however, if you look at the words on the page there is only a general relation between what the child is saying and the words that are printed. In the final phases the child begins to pay attention to the print on the page. At first, the child goes between using print and storytelling, but in the final stage the child reads conventionally using the print.

This typology helps us realize that the child learns many important aspects of reading from handling books and storybook reading in the early years. The change from oral language to book-like language clearly shows that the child is learning something about the language of books. And the ultimate shift in focus from pictures to print shows that the child is gradually building a notion about the relation between stories and print. The use of the word *emergent* to describe these early stages of reading highlights the fact that learning to read is a complex process that may begin long before the child reaches school.

Attending to Print

Much is covered in the final two phases of Sulzby's typology, attending to print and reading conventionally. How does a child learn to attend to print and, furthermore, to make sense of it? Some children learn how to turn print into words without much instruction and some children do not learn despite a great deal of instruction. Learning to turn print into stories and words is complex because there are at least four ways to read words: (1) by sight using the visual code, (2) by letter-sound decoding using the sound code, (3) by analogy (a combination of the sound and visual codes), and (4) by contextual guessing. Words read by sight (or the visual code) are identified by matching visual representations to information stored in memory from previous encounters with the word. Reading words by letter-sound decoding (using the sound code) involves remembering the sounds that go with the letters of the word and blending them together to get to the representation of the word in memory. Reading words by analogy means using familiar words to identify unfamiliar ones (combining the sound and visual codes). For example a child might figure out *host* by remembering how to pronounce *post* and substituting the beginning *h* sound for the beginning *p* sound. And finally, sometimes the context around the word is sufficient to identify the word. (See Chapter 2, p. 29 for further discussion of these terms.) Skilled readers usually identify words by sight (using the visual code), but when they are not familiar with a word they can use any of the other methods and sometimes a combination of them to figure it out.

Given that skilled readers recognize most words by sight it would seem that teaching children to recognize words by sight (sometimes called the whole-word method) would make sense. However, remember that skilled readers and beginning readers may do things differently. Ehri and her colleagues (Gaskins, Ehri, Cress, O'Hara, & Donnelly, 1997) have shown that beginning readers are likely to pass through at least four stages as they develop a sight vocabulary: prealphabetic, partial alphabetic, full alphabetic, and consolidated alphabetic. In the prealphabetic stages children identify words according to visual features. For example, they may remember *look* because the *o*'s in the middle look like eyes, or they may remember a thumbprint or a stray ink mark on a particular flash card. Usually they select one visual cue and ignore the rest. At this stage the child does not know enough about letters, the sounds in words, and the relations between the two to do anything else.

However, this system breaks down quickly. Many words have double *o*'s in the middle (*book, crook, brook, cook, nook,* and *shook*) but not all of them are *look*. Similarly, if there is a thumbprint or stray ink mark on one flashcard, there are likely to be marks on several others as well. Evidence indicates that once a child learns some letters and realizes that words are made up of sounds (this realization is called phonemic awareness), they discover that letters and sounds can be used to help them remember words. For example, a child may look at the word *cartoon* and remember that it begins with the sound of *c* and ends with the sound of *n*. In other words they remember some of the sounds and letters. Ehri designates this as the partial alphabetic phase.

Although the partial alphabetic phase is more efficient than using just visual cues, it too has its drawbacks. There are many words that begin with *c* and quite a few that begin with *c* and end with *n* such as *can, crown, caution, caption,* and *column.* This inefficiency prompts the child to move to the full alphabetic phase in which entire word is analyzed for letters and sounds. Once the children can do a full alphabetic analysis and begin to encounter words with similar parts such as *book, cook, look, took, rook, nook,* and *hook,* they begin to consolidate the sounds that occur in familiar patterns. For example, *ook* becomes a unit that they identify automatically without going through the separate sounds. These larger units are easier to use than those that go with each letter because they are more consistent. It is also faster to access them as unit than to analyze letter by letter. Sight words or words that children know by memorizing how they look are consolidated units.

EMERGENT, BEGINNING, AND TRANSITION READERS

Sulzby's phases were designed to describe emergent readers. What happens to development in the beginning and transition phases? The chart in Table 2 summarizes what readers from each phase know about five critical areas of reading and writing development: word identification, word recognition, comprehension, fluency, and writing.

Word identification refers to use of the sound code, visual code, and context to figure out unknown words. Emergent readers discover the sound code and begin to understand the relations between letters and their sounds. By the end of the emergent phase they can usually use beginning sounds along with contextual information to figure out words. They also can substitute one beginning consonant for another, for example they can substitute *p* for *h* in *host* and say "post." They recognize common endings like *-ed, -s,* and *-ing.* Beginning readers have developed a good understanding of the sound system and know or are learning the letter-sound relations

Table 2
Reading and Writing Development for Emergent, Beginning, and Transition Readers

	Emergent	Beginning	Transition
Word Identification	letter-sound relations for consonants; use initial letter with context to to pronounce words.	letter-sound relations for consonants and vowels combine sounds and context to pronounce words.	use word structure, Greek and Latin roots to figure out pronunciation and meaning of words.
Word Recognition	recognize 200–300 most frequent words by end of phase.	recognize most words in speaking vocabulary by end of phase.	expand sight vocabulary beyond spoken vocabulary through reading.
Comprehension	discover that reading is talk written down; learn how stories are told and and understood through print.	understand expository and narrative texts about familiar concepts.	read range of expository and narrative texts and learn new concepts.
Fluency	read expressively at 60 words per minute.	read expressively at 80–100 words per minute; begin transition to silent reading.	vary rate according to difficulty of material; become more efficient at silent reading; silent reading rates are 150–200 words per minute.
Writing	understand that words are made up of sounds that can be represented with letters; spell some common words.	expand number of words they can spell; write about familiar topics and use familiar forms; experiment with several genres.	expand number of words they can spell; increase length and complexity; expand genres, combine information from multiple sources.

involved in vowels. They recognize common letter patterns such as *-ake* and *-ain* (which are called phonograms), and they can segment multisyllable words and pronounce their parts. They are able to combine this sound code knowledge with information from context to figure out unknown words.

Transition readers are beginning to learn word structure patterns such as Greek and Latin root words, suffixes, and prefixes. They can combine this knowledge with contextual information to arrive at both the pronunciation and meaning of words.

Word recognition refers to the process of recognizing common words through the visual code. Emergent readers work to achieve instant recognition of about 200 to 300 common words whose meaning they know because they are already using them in their spoken language. The task of beginning readers is to expand the number of instantly recognized words to a number more consistent with those in their spoken vocabulary. Transition readers are beginning to expand their sight vocabulary to words that they learn through text and that are not first represented in their spoken language.

Comprehension refers to understanding. Emergent readers' task is to discover that reading is talk written down and that it has a meaning or a message. They discover this gradually as they interact with their environment and learn that certain symbols, such as the *stop* on stop signs, appear in many places and mean the same thing each time. They also become aware of the family's use of grocery lists and memo pads for messages. They learn how stories are told and understood through print and begin to use story language such as *Once upon a time* or *The End*. Beginning readers are able to understand narrative or expository texts made up mainly of familiar concepts. Because they are still working on putting all their reading knowledge together, it is hard for them to learn new information when they are reading. They are working too hard at the reading. Transition readers, on the other hand, are capable of learning new information from print. They can follow a logical argument and understand increasingly complex sentences and paragraphs. They begin to appreciate the literary qualities of text such as repeating patterns and figurative and poetic language.

Fluency refers to the expressiveness of reading. Emergent readers can be expected to achieve a rate of 60 words per minute. Their voices will follow expected patterns of intonation—rising at the end for questions or to express surprise, and pausing at commas. They will be much more fluent in patterned material and in material that they are rereading. Beginning readers are developing skill in automatic and smooth processing of print. Oral reading improves in speed to about 80 to 100 words per minute and their initial readings often sound more expressive with appropriate grouping of phrases and clauses and dramatic inflections. They also begin to process text silently. Transition readers vary their rates of reading depending on the complexity of the material. They read simple stories quickly and easily but slow their rates for difficult material. Their reading patterns are more similar to adults who read faster silently than orally. Their silent reading rates increase to 100 to 200 words per minute and are faster than their oral rates.

In writing, emergent readers are beginning to understand that words are composed of sounds and that there are letters to represent those sounds. They draw and write stories such as the ones displayed in Figures 8 and 9. By the end of the emergent phase they are able to write readable text. They can spell common words such as Mommy, Daddy, and love. Emergent readers write mostly about their own lives and the people they know. Beginning readers expand the number of words they can write with conventional spelling, their stories increase in length and complexity, and they may experiment with several genres such as nonfiction, fiction and poetry. Beginning readers' stories are similar to Randy's Wacky Waters story (see page 95 of *Variability Not Disability*). Transition readers expand the number of words they can write and they are beginning to combine information from several sources in more complex ways in their texts. For example, they may combine information from several books about Egypt to develop a piece about mummies. Their reading and writing repertoires expand and influence one another.

What Must Reading Tutors Know?

Reading tutors need to know a great deal, some of which we have covered. They need to know what tutoring looks like (Chapter 1), they need to know how skilled reading operates (Chapter 2), and they need to know how reading and writing develop (this chapter). You also will need to know the information in the remaining chapters of this book. However, because reading and writing development is so important, reading tutors need to know the letter-sound relations that characterize the English writing system and the high-frequency words that make up much of English text. This information is summarized in Tables 3, 4, and 5.

Perhaps even more critical is that tutors recognize when words are consistent with the general patterns of English writing and when they are not. For example, *gave, save, nave, Dave, rave, brave, cave, pave,* and *wave* all have a long *a* sound—the sound you hear when you say the letter name *a*. These words are consistent with a somewhat general pattern in English spelling that says when words end in the *-vce*

Table 3
Common Letter-Sound Relationships

Consonants

b boy, *c* cat (sometimes *circle*), *d* dog, *f* fat, *g* goat, (sometimes *gym*), *h* hat, *j* jam, *k* kite, *l* log, *m* mom, *n* nap, *p* pat, *q* quiet, *r* rat, *s* sock, *t* tool, *v* vase, *w* wing, *x* exit, *y* yellow, *z* zoo.

Consonant Blends (consonants whose sounds blend together)

br bread, *bl* blood, *cr* cream, *cl* clean, *dr* drive, *fr* from, *gr* growl, *gl* glow, *pr* pray, *pl* play, *sl* sleep, *st* stone, *str* street, *tr* tree.

Consonant Digraphs (consonants that do not blend individual sounds)

sh sheep, *ch* cherry, *th* the and thing, *wh* whale.

Vowels

Short Vowel Sounds

a at, *e* Ed, *i* it, *o* on, *u* up.

Long Vowel Sounds

a ate, *e* eat, *I* I, *o* oak, *u* use.

Common Vowel Patterns

CVC hat, get, fit, hot, nut	VCE gave, scene, fine, home, tune
VVC train, boat, beat	CV be, hi, go

Common Vowel Pairs

ai rain	*ee*, *ea*, *ie* teen, team, believe
oa boat	*oi*, *oy* oil, boy
au, *aw* author, saw	

Common Word Patterns (phonograms)

-ack -all -ain -ake -ale -ame -an -ank -ap -ash -at -ate -aw -ay -eat -ell-est -ice -ick -ide -ight -ill -in -ine -ing -ink -ip -ir -ock -oke -op -ore -or- -uck -ug -ump -unk

From Adams, M.J. (1990). *Beginning to Read: Thinking and Learning About Print* (pp. 321–322). Cambridge, MA: Massachusetts Institute of Technology Press. Adapted by permission.

pattern (v for vowel, c for consonant, e for final *e*), the vowel says it name. This is true in all the listed examples. In each word *a* says /a/ like its name. However, *have* is not consistent with this pattern, and *have* is far more frequent than the words that are consistent. When a child is having trouble with *have* therefore, it is not appro-

Table 4
Commonly Taught Rules for Sounding Multisyllabic Words

1. Break off common prefixes and suffixes.

unlawful:	un	law	ful

2. Make sure there is one vowel sound in each word part.

antivivisectionist:	an	ti	viv	i	sec	tion	ist

3. Divide between consonants

apple:	ap	ple	sister:	sis	ter

4. When you have a single consonant between two vowels, first try dividing before the consonant and giving the long sound. If that does not make sense try dividing after the consonant and making the short sound.

robin:	ro	bin	rob	in
tiger:	ti	ger	tig	er

priate to tell the child to "sound it out." Although the /h/ and the /v/ carry important and consistent letter-sound information the /a/ and the /e/ are traitors. In this case the child needs to combine various routes using the sounds of the *h* and the *v* and the sense of the text to help him or her realize that the word is *have*. One of the more treacherous aspects of English spelling is that the more frequently a word occurs in print the more likely it is to violate common spelling patterns. Look at the sight word chart in Table 5 that lists common sight words. Note the number of rule violators including *a, the, have, some, been, want, any,* and *come*.

Finally, I must place another caution here because having said that letter-sound relations and instant recognition of high-frequency words are important, I also must say that letter-sound relations and recognition of sight words are simply a *part*, albeit an important part, of the reading process.

FOR THE SUPERVISOR

Ehri's claims that children must move through a full alphabetic phase to develop a sight vocabulary are very important because they suggest that readers must learn to use the alphabetic code in spite of the fact that skilled readers recognize most words by sight and do not sound out most words as they read. There is considerable

Table 5
Common Sight Words

the	day	were	take	found	sat
and	at	ask	eat	lady	stay
a	have	back	body	soon	each
I	your	now	school	ran	ever
to	mother	friend	house	dear	until
said	come	cry	morning	man	shout
you	not	oh	yes	better	mama
he	like	Mr.	after	through	use
it	then	bed	never	stop	turn
in	get	an	or	still	thought
was	when	very	self	fast	papa
she	thing	where	try	next	lot
for	do	play	has	only	blue
that	too	let	always	am	bath
is	want	long	over	began	mean
his	did	here	again	head	sit
but	could	how	side	keep	together
they	good	make	thank	teacher	best
my	this	big	why	sure	brother
of	don't	from	who	says	feel
on	little	put	saw	ride	floor
me	if	read	mom	pet	wait
all	just	them	kid	hurry	tomorrow
be	baby	as	give	hand	surprise
go	way	Miss	around	hard	shop
can	there	any	by	push	run
with	every	right	Mrs.	our	own
one	went	nice	off	their	
her	father	other	sister	watch	
what	had	well	find	because	
we	see	old	fun	door	
him	dog	night	more	us	
no	home	may	while	should	
so	down	about	tell	room	
out	got	think	sleep	pull	
up	would	new	made	great	
are	time	know	first	gave	
will	love	help	say	does	
look	walk	grand	took	car	
some	came	boy	dad	ball	

Adapted from Eeds, M. (1985). "Bookwords: Using a beginning word list of high frequency words from children's literature K–3." *The Reading Teacher, 38*, p. 420.

disagreement about this in the reading field, however Ehri (1991) has produced and cited several kinds of evidence to support her claims. Some of them involve teaching people to read two kinds of nonsense words—words in which letters are related to sounds and words in which there is no relation between letters and sounds. For example, for *chair* the former might be *CHR* and the later *XND*. If sight-word reading does *not* involve using letter-sound decoding then people learning these words, with many exposures should read both with equal skill. That is not what happens, however. Brooks (1977), whose study is cited by Ehri, found that for the first 200 trials the sound spellings were read more slowly than random spellings. In the second 200 pronunciations, however, the sound spellings were read more quickly than the random spellings. This pattern suggests that the readers initially were relating the sounds to letters in letter spellings and that this took some extra time. However, in the second 200 pronunciations, the faster reading time suggests that somehow the readers had combined the letters into a unified representation that was pronounced more quickly. This suggests a process of consolidation of sound spellings such as the one that Ehri proposes.

That letter-sound decoding and its prerequisites are important correlates of skilled reading is well established. Letter-name knowledge and phonemic awareness scores in kindergarten are very strong predictors of reading achievement. Ehri summarizes her 1991 argument by saying the following:

> Findings of various studies indicate that phonological recoding skill is necessary for proficient sight word reading. Sight words are stored in memory by forming access routes linking spellings to the phonological structure of words in memory. This type of sight word reading is qualitatively different from logographic (prealphabetic) which characterizes how immature readers read words. (p. 405)

Several cautions are important here. First, although letter-sound decoding is very important and we can demonstrate it is related to skilled readers' sight-word reading, it is not the only way to identify words. Readers also can identify words by analogy and by using surrounding context. Second, the fact that young readers need to learn letter-sound relations says nothing about how letter-sound relations should be taught. Indeed it does not even mean that they should be taught. Many children may learn these principles and relations on their own. However, if children do not know how to do this by the time they begin reading instruction, they should be taught in some way.

Knowing how reading and writing develop is a major concern of tutors. They are often insecure because they feel like they do not know anything about reading and writing and what is "normal" at particular ages. Provide tutors with many writing samples and videotapes of children reading at various points in the progression. The more examples tutors see, the more confident they will become about their judgments of children's development, and the more likely they will be to make good judgments about what comes next for individual children.

Chapter 4

General Principles of Tutoring

TUTORING IS *more effective than group instruction for many reasons.* These include more time spent reading, immediate feedback, more tailored teaching, more extended interaction between tutor and child, and strong positive emotional relationships. Researchers and educators are not really sure which of these factors are most important and account for tutoring effectiveness, but descriptions of good tutoring sessions suggest that all of them are present. Tutoring effectiveness depends on complex relations among these factors and others. This chapter offers a few general principles of good tutoring. The principles are grouped under two headings: establishing a warm, supportive environment and scaffolding children's learning.

ESTABLISHING A WARM, SUPPORTIVE ENVIRONMENT

Although there is no definitive research, descriptions of tutoring suggest that good tutoring sessions have a strong positive emotional tone (Juel, 1996). This tone is established when the tutor gets to know the child, gives specific praise, keeps the session moving, and enjoys reading and writing.

Get to Know the Child

Getting to know the child is the tutor's first important task. Although knowledge of the child grows over time, the first few sessions may be crucial to setting the tone of the relationship. Devoting time in early sessions to learn about the child is essential.

Talk* with *the child not* to *him or her. Sometimes adults and teachers use a special tone with children. They ask many "known answer" questions—questions to which adults already know the answers. A first-grade teacher might drill children on colors: "And what color is this?" with emphasis on "what color" and a rapidly rising intonation on "this." The stress and intonation say clearly, "I am the teacher and you are the student. You must give the right answer, and I, the teacher, know what the right answer is." Adults often slip into this mode of talking down to students. Nothing can be more counterproductive if what you really want is to learn about the child. Interactions should sound like conversations, not lessons.

Learn to take the short turn. The best way to learn about a child is to listen to him or her, but this is more difficult than it seems. Both children and adults are used to adults talking and asking questions while children listen and give short answers. There are several techniques you can use to break this pattern. You can

- ask open-ended questions,
- wait for the child to talk,
- be genuinely interested in what the child has to say,
- use positive nonverbal gestures,
- make short comments, and
- repeat the child's last few words with rising intonation.

Open-ended questions are questions that cannot be responded to with one-word answers. For example, rather than asking, "Did you like...?" which can be answered simply with a yes or no, ask, "What did you think about...?" Another open-ended technique is to make a simple statement, "I really liked the _____," and wait for the child to take his or her turn. Your pause indicates that the child must speak, and the fact that you have not asked a specific question gives the child the opportunity to say what is on his or her mind.

However, even open-ended questions will draw brief nonanswers unless you wait for a reply. When children do not immediately answer our questions, we have a tendency to jump in, asking more questions and sometimes even answering our own questions. We sometimes "help" children by finishing their sentences. Because long silences are uncomfortable we fill them with our adult talk. Waiting is probably the most important thing we can do to signal our interest. Sometimes we need to wait as long as 5 to 10 seconds. It seems like an eternity! Remember, however, that the child usually understands the basic rules of conversation. He or she knows that if no one is talking and you had the last turn, it is his or her turn to participate. He or she will talk, given the chance. Another time waiting is effective is when the child pauses. If we maintain eye contact and simply wait, the child will read it as a signal to continue.

Listening attentively will show the child we are genuinely interested in him or her. We can use positive nonverbal gestures such as head nodding, smiling, or chuckling to show our enjoyment. Short comments such as "Really?" "Oh?" or "What else?" also show your attention. Children will say a surprising amount if the tutor simply says, "mmm" or "uh huh" when it is his or her turn in the conversation. Another strategy for tutors is to repeat the child's last few words with rising intonation which signals the expectation that the child will continue. All of these strategies will help you get children talking and if you listen to what the child says you will learn a lot about him or her.

The following dialogue is an example of a lengthy interaction that I had with a usually quiet child as he answered a question from an interest inventory that usually involves only a short response.

1. *Cathy*: Matt, who's a good reader that you know?

2. *Matt*: Carl Walters.

3. *Cathy*: Carl Walters? [repeating with a rising intonation]

4. *Matt*: He's a second grader.

5. *Cathy*: Um hm. [short encouraging comment]

6. *Matt*: He's also my best friend. When he was in first grade they said he could read at a sixth-grade level.

7. *Cathy*:   Wow. That's pretty impressive isn't it?

8. *Matt*:   Um hm. (pause) [wait time] That was when I was in his class. He was in the red group. I was in the blue group.

9. *Cathy*:   He was in the red group. You were in the blue group. [repetition with rising intonation]

10. *Matt*:   That was the highest group.

11. *Cathy*:   The red group? [clarifying question]

12. *Matt*:   Hm.

13. *Cathy*:   And the blue group. What was the blue group? [clarifying question]

14. *Matt*:   Lowest.

15. *Cathy*:   Lowest. [repetition with rising intonation]

16. *Matt*:   And I'm still in it.

17. *Cathy*:   You're still there? [repetition with rising intonation]

18. *Matt*:   Well I used to be, I used to be. I think I went from the blue group, I mean the red group to the green group...I mean yellow group. I started at the yellow group and then I went to blue group and then I think I went to the green group and now I'm in blue group cause there isn't a green group.

19. *Cathy*:   Say that again. I didn't quite get that sequence. That was complicated. First you started out in the...

20. *Matt*:   yellow group.

21. *Cathy*:   Yellow group. And what group was that? [repetition and clarifying question]

22. *Matt*:   Second to the highest.

59

23. *Cathy*:   Second to the highest, and then... [repetition and encouraging comment]

24. *Matt*:   and then I went to the blue group. Lowest.

25. *Cathy*:   Lowest. [repetition with rising intonation]

26. *Matt*:   And then they found a new group called the green group, and then I went to the green group, and now I'm in second grade, but there isn't a green group, so I gotta go back and be in the blue group.

27. *Cathy*:   How do you feel about bein' in that blue group?

28. *Matt*:   (makes a rude noise with a thumbs down sign.)

At least half of my 14 turns involved repeating what Matt said. I also made statements and a brief request for clarification. Through the first nine turns of the conversation I recall using strategies consciously. In turn 3, I purposely repeated the child's name, and in turn 5, I purposely responded with "um hm." In turn 7, I made a comment about what he said in turn 6, and in turn 8 I consciously used wait time. My repetition in turn 9 also was conscious. However, after turn 9, I was not conscious of using conversational strategies. Matt was telling me fascinating things about his reading history, so the requests for clarification and short repetitions were a consequence of being genuinely interested in what he had to say.

Build reading and writing activities around the child's interests.

Building tutoring activities around children's interests is another way to become better acquainted with them. Children's interests usually become obvious as you listen to them, but if you are having trouble discovering your student's interests, there are many informal interest inventories that you can use as a starting point. Offering a child choice in reading and writing activities can reveal much about him or her. Writing activities can build easily on a child's interests because in one-on-one sessions he or she always can choose what he or she wants to write about. Reading activities may be a little more difficult because finding appropriately easy books about topics of interest to the child can be a challenge. However, the amount of children's literature has increased dramatically in recent years. (The lists at the end of *Variability Not Disability* tell you how to find appropriate books for children.) In addition, you can offer your child a choice among appropriate reading materials and you can read books that you and the child have written together. If the child *wants* to read, the battle to teach him or her how is half won.

Be culturally sensitive. Cultural sensitivity is imperative. Even if you come from the same cultural and ethnic background as the child, there may be differences between your views of family, community, and the world. If you are from a different ethnic and cultural background there most certainly will be differences in your views. Sometimes differences about what the "right" answer is are really differences about the worlds you come from.

Cultural differences were a factor in Cynthia Lewis' (1993) interactions with a child. She was working with him on a fable about an upper-class crane who invites a lowly pelican to tea. The pelican is very sloppy and messy and seems oblivious of his bad manners. The moral the author assigns the fable is "When one is a social failure, the reasons are as clear as day." The reader clearly is supposed to identify with the crane. However, the little boy with whom Lewis was working thought the moral was, "Give people a chance." During the tutoring session Lewis did not see how the child had arrived at this moral, and with questions she tried to move him toward the author's moral. However, after listening to a tape recording of this session, she realized that the child had seen the fable from the pelican's point of view, and had even identified the pelican with his mother. Lewis concluded that as a middle-class teacher working with this working-class child, she had made assumptions about the world that he did not share. Because she identified with the crane as the author had intended, she interpreted the child's plausible alternative as wrong.

If we explore fully why the child says what he or she says, we can be sensitive to differences and avoid incorrect assumptions. Rather than pushing the child toward the crane's perspective, Lewis suggested that she needed to back off. She needed to listen more closely to what the child was saying instead of responding to what he was not saying. The difference between right and wrong answers can be a matter of perspective. Tutors must be careful to discover and to honor the child's perspective.

Give Specific Praise

The one-on-one tutoring session is ideally suited to praising children. You can tell them regularly what they are doing well and that you like it. Because you are working with just one child, you can be very specific in your praise and the more specific you are, the better the child will understand what it is you want him or her to do.

Be positive and accepting.   The general tone you set should be positive and accepting. Children like to be praised, so if you begin each session telling the child something specific you like about him or her or about what he or she is doing, you will get off to a positive start. This start will lead to more positive behavior and will set a positive tone. Children will occasionally do things that require correction. They may refuse to sit at the table or do any work, or they may strike at you or others. In these situations, be very specific about what you object to, why you object to it, and the behavior you expect in its place. Make it clear it is the child's actions, not the child himself or herself that you object to. As soon as the child moves toward compliance, give praise and hopefully you will be moving toward a positive tone.

Be honest.   Children sense when adults praise them without actually believing that their behavior is praiseworthy. To avoid embarrassing a child, a tutor often will act as if an answer is correct when it is in fact wrong. This confuses the child. If an answer is wrong, do not be afraid to acknowledge that it is wrong, but be quick to point out the praiseworthy aspects of the answer. For example, in the model lesson on page 7 in Chapter 1, the child said, "What makes" when the text said, "Who made." I did not call attention to the miscues because they made sense and had appropriate beginning sounds. However, when the child asked, "Is this right?" I responded by saying, "I like what you are doing. Because you looked at the print and you noticed that it's not quite right." The praise was honest. I did like what he was doing and the answer was not quite right. The praise was specific and encouraged the student to look carefully at print, something that was absolutely essential for him to learn to read.

Keep the Session Moving

Many lessons and tutoring sessions get bogged down. Sometimes tutors have trouble moving from one activity to another, other times the child cannot do what the tutor or teacher expects, and sometimes the tutor dominates the session.

Be organized.   Not knowing what is coming next or fumbling as you move from activity to activity can create a sense of disorganization that is frustrating for the child. While you are searching for materials and trying to remember what to do, the child has time on his or her hands. It is important to have your materials well organized so you can move smoothly from one activity to the next. An agenda written on a chart or chalkboard can give the child a sense of the overall session and how you are moving within it. Checking off activities as you complete them gives the session a sense of forward motion.

Know when to quit. Many lessons and tutoring sessions lose momentum when children cannot do what the tutor or teacher expects. As the lesson continues, the tone becomes increasingly negative. Sometimes tutors get stuck looking for the answer to a particular question. When the child cannot answer, the tutor begins asking a series of questions, each question getting simpler and simpler, in hopes that the child will answer correctly. Often the child cannot give the answer and the tutor ends up giving it. This process takes a long time and keeps the child in a failing situation. I have heard tapes of student teachers working with a supervisor who wants them to come up with a right answer that they simply do not know. I chuckled when one of these students asked, "Why don't you just *tell me* the answer?" This is a very good question, and although I would not recommend telling all the answers all the time, it is acceptable to tell the answers some of the time, particularly if the child shows signs of frustration. When a child is frustrated, the atmosphere of the session quickly loses its positive emotional tone.

Likewise, if you get into a book or an activity that is too hard, it is often better to simply stop and move on. With a difficult book the tutor can simply take over and read it to the child, or say, "I think this is too hard, let's put it aside and we'll come back to it later in the year." With a difficult activity it is probably best to just abandon it by saying, "I don't think this is working very well. Let's do something else."

Do not dominate the story with your teaching. When you are reading easy books you should do no teaching at all. When you are reading difficult books, your focus should be on getting the information. In instructional-level books you should do some teaching, but not at every opportunity that presents itself. You should choose a few good opportunities that will help the child learn something very important that he or she needs to know. If you take every opportunity you will dominate the lesson, destroy the story, and the child constantly will be struggling. (See Chapter 9 for further discussion on how to make decisions about when to teach.)

Enjoy Reading and Writing Yourself

It is important that you convey your love of reading and writing to a child. Children want to be like the adults they admire. Emulating adults is a strong motivational force. If you are positive and happy about reading and writing, they will want to be positive and happy about it too.

Talk about your own reading and writing. Talking about your reading and writing in tutoring sessions is one way to let children know how reading and writing are important in your life. There are many ways for you to convey this importance to the child you tutor, such as sharing a funny story, talking about a well-loved fictional character, commenting on receiving a response to a letter to the editor that you wrote, or sharing your planner and showing how you use it to organize yourself. Talking about a favorite author, as I did on page 15 of Chapter 1 when Margaret selected a Judith Viorst book is another way to share your enthusiasm. With all children you can use examples of material you have written or read to model and demonstrate what they need to learn.

For example, when I was trying to explain the concept of easy, "just-right," and "dream" books to children, I brought in a Barbara Taylor Bradford novel, *Some Tame Gazelle* by Barbara Pym (1984), and an issue of a professional reading journal titled *Reading Research Quarterly*. I talked about each one and read short excerpts explaining why the Bradford book was easy for me, why *Some Tame Gazelle* was just right, and why some articles in *Reading Research Quarterly* were dream level.

On another occasion I shared my experience figuring out unknown words in Mark Helprin's book *Refiner's Fire*. I came across the words *slurred elisions* in the sentence *Their [arriving and departing ships] progress fit the slurred elisions of the brass, drums and woodwinds from the gardens, and their wakes seemed to freeze on the surface.* I know that *slurred* means run together, but I was not sure about *elisions*. Because the previous sentence had identified the musicians as jazz players from New Orleans and Chicago I thought perhaps it meant the way trombones sometimes slide through many notes as they go from one note to another instead of moving crisply to each note in between. I also wondered if the word was related to *ellipsis* which means leaving things out. I really was not sure, but I knew that this small sentence was not critical to my understanding of the novel and so I read on. I knew that if I came across the word again I would learn more about it, and if it were really important to my understanding I would look it up. I eventually did look it up and discovered that it means leaving things out. I used this example to show the children how using the context and what I know about the world and about similar words helps me figure out words. The fact that I shared the example demonstrates that I like reading and figuring things out for myself.

Talk about why you like the stories the child reads and writes. Talking about why you like the stories the child reads and writes is another way to convey the importance of reading and writing and of the particular things the child is reading and writing. Often children who are struggling with reading and writing do not believe that what they read and write is valuable or important. Because their literacy skills are developed after talking and thinking skills, and because they are aware of the differences between what they can read and write and what other children their age can read and write, they often view their own reading and writing with disdain. For example, children often will equate easy books with boring books and insist they do not *want* to read anything they *can* read because it is boring. Although this may be true to some extent, you can challenge the idea that easy means boring. Think about your responses to very easy books. Often there is a clever twist to the ending, or the simplicity of the story emphasizes some universally important themes such as Gruff's message that cleverness can overcome power in *The Three Billy Goats Gruff* (Asbjornsen, 1973). In addition, illustrations in easy books are often works of art. Similarly, children, particularly those who will only use words that they can spell, often feel that their own stories are not worthwhile. It is therefore very important to tell children what you honestly like and enjoy about their reading and writing.

give just the right amount of assistance

SCAFFOLD THE CHILD'S LEARNING

Scaffolding means providing the level of support that a child needs at a particular time and then gradually reducing the amount of support until the child can operate independently. It refers to the way adults give just the right amount of assistance to help children learn. Children learn a lot by working and playing alongside adults who are going about the business of daily living. For example, think about how adults teach babies to walk. They scaffold, providing support that the child needs: first two hands that support the child's entire weight as they encourage foot movement (sometimes even moving the child's feet!); gradually supporting less of the child's weight by reducing the support to a finger on each hand, to one hand, then one finger; and finally encouraging the child to cross short distances without support. They also constantly praise the child's attempts and encourage the child when he or she falters. Certainly they do not criticize the child and try to get them to take steps in particular ways or particular lengths. (See Chapter 6 of *Variability Not Disability* for an extended explanation of scaffolding.)

Model and Explain

The first stage in scaffolding is to provide good models accompanied by explanations. Infants are surrounded by good models of walking. As we begin to teach them, we accompany our physical movements with related words: Put one foot first and follow with the other. In reading, there are many skills a child must learn. Modeling and explanation are the first steps in teaching them.

Examples in word identification. Some children do not understand immediately how to figure out words by combining information they get from the letters with the meaning they are getting from the text as they read. Modeling with explanation is a simple way to show them how to do this. Often these explanations start with, "If I were having trouble figuring out that word, I would think about what they are saying or doing and then I would ask myself, 'What word that starts with the ___ sound would make sense here?'" For example, suppose a child were having trouble with the word *jeans* in the sentence *I packed my sweatshirts and jeans*. I might say, "Hmm. He's packing his clothes because he's going to run away from home. And he already put his sweatshirts in. What would he put in that starts with 'jjjjjjuh jjuh' I packed my sweatshirts and 'jjj' oh jeans—jeans would make sense here and it matches the other letters too." I solved the problem and explained how I solved it.

Examples in comprehension. Word-recognition skills are not all we need to model. Comprehension is always the goal of reading, and sometimes we do not understand the content even though we know all the words. For example, on the same page of *Refiner's Fire* I mentioned earlier, the author talks about the musicians liking Israel because it reminds them of a more gracious time in America. The sentence reads: *It reminded them of trolleys (although in Haifa there are no trolleys), and the old fashioned graces they had known before America put on its skin.* I'm not sure what the author means when he writes *before America put on its skin*, but I know this story takes place right after World War II and I think that jazz had its golden age in the 1920s and 1930s. Maybe musicians in that period did not feel the effects of segregation in Chicago and New Orleans. So perhaps what he means is that the United States put on its white skin and then the black musicians were not as free and happy as they were previously.

Children need to know that texts do not always make sense immediately and that it is important to think about your reading as you go. Making sense of text is a reader's job, a job that is particularly important for struggling readers who often become so focused on pronouncing words that they really do not pay much attention to what the text means. When children are struggling to make sense of their reading you can model the processes you use to make sense by talking out loud about how you might figure out the particular text they are working on.

Give the Right Amount of Help

Learning usually does not happen all at once. Rather it takes many tries and a great deal of practice to learn something. Even though children understand the basic idea of what they should do when they read and are able to do it sometimes, there are times when they do not. This inconsistency probably happens because coordinating all the processes and strategies is difficult. Children need to practice until some of the strategies become automatic. In the period when the child understands and is learning, it is important to give the right kinds and amounts of help.

Practicing Strategies With Your Student. An example from SRP demonstrates this fact. The tutor, Sandy, was encouraging Karl to skip an unknown word, go on, and then come back to it. Karl had difficulty hearing the sounds in words. However, he was convinced that he should figure out *all* words by sounding them out. He often spent 30 seconds to a minute or more sounding out words, and he often failed. Sandy thought Karl needed to learn additional strategies. She had introduced skipping a word and returning to it later in a minilesson. She modeled and explained how this strategy could help Karl figure out words he did not know. However, Karl was not convinced, and continued to rely on sounding out every word. Early in a session on June 13, Karl read Ruth Brown's *A Dark, Dark Tale* (1981). He had just turned the page to read the sentence *Across the passage there was a dark, dark curtain* and he was stuck on the word *across*.

Sandy:	What's something you can do if you're stuck on a word?
Karl:	Look at the pictures?
Sandy:	Are the pictures going to help this time?
Karl:	Uh, no.
Sandy:	If you're stuck on that word, what else can you do besides the pictures?
Karl:	(pause) I don't know.
Sandy:	How about skipping it?

Karl:	...the passage was a dark, dark curtain. (pause) Across?
Sandy:	Good! How did you figure that out?
Karl:	I don't know. It just came to me.
Sandy:	Uhmm. You skipped it and then it was easier for you to figure out when you came back.

Notice that Sandy began by asking the child what he could do. She did not jump in immediately and tell him, because she thought he might know. However, when it became clear that he was not going to come up with the strategy, she suggested that he skip it. When he used the strategy successfully, she asked him how he did it, in order to make sure he was conscious of the strategy he used. He did not give a very complete explanation, so she told him what he had done.

On June 17, Karl was reading *The Cow That Went Oink* by Bernard Most (1990). He was reading the sentence *The horse, the donkey, and the sheep thought this was very funny* and he was stuck on *thought*.

Sandy:	What could you do?
Karl:	Oh...skip it...that this was very funny.
Sandy:	So what did they do? After you skip it come back now.
Karl:	Thought this was very funny.

Notice that this time when Sandy asked, Karl came up with the idea of skipping the word, but he did not go back. So Sandy helped by prompting him with the rest of the strategy.

On June 24, Karl was reading *Animals Should Definitely Not Wear Clothing* by Judi Barrett (1970). He was reading the part of a sentence *because it might make life hard for a hen* and he was stuck on *life*. He paused for a long time.

Sandy:	You're stuck on that word....What could you do? (long pause) What are you doing right now to figure out that word?
Karl:	Thinking
Sandy:	OK...How about if you would skip it?
Karl:	Oh! OK.
Sandy:	Because it might make...blank...
Karl:	... hard for a hen...life. It might make life hard for a hen.

Sandy:	Good! We skipped and came back and it was easy to figure out that word.

Even though in previous lessons Karl had demonstrated that he knew about the skip-and-go-back strategy, he was not using it. His tutor was careful to check with him about what he was actually doing as he sat in silence. Once again she suggested the strategy and she even got him started by reading the beginning of the sentence and saying "blank" in place of the word. When he got the word, she again explained what he did.

On July 1, Karl was reading the book *Clifford Goes to Hollywood* by Norman Bridwell (1985). Sandy began the session with a review of the strategy.

Sandy:	If you get stuck on a word, what is the very first thing you can try today?
Karl:	Sound it out.
Sandy:	OK. You can sound it out, but what might be a better thing to do even before that?
Karl:	Look at the pictures.
Sandy:	You could look at the pictures. What else?
Karl:	Go before it?
Sandy:	Go before it...go back and reread or what else? (pause) skip it and go... (pause)
Karl:	on.
Sandy:	Try and think about doing the skip and go on one right away instead of sounding it out.

Notice that even after several positive examples Karl had not adopted the strategy. It was not because Karl did not understand. The fact that he could finish the strategy with "on" and had offered the strategy in previous sessions suggests he knew and understood the strategy. Evidently the sounding out strategy had been taught and reinforced so strongly and was so automatic that integrating a new strategy was really difficult for Karl. Later in the session Karl was reading the text *There were a lot of parties. Clifford got tired of them but they said movie stars have to go to a lot of parties.*

69

Karl:	There were a lot of p...par...parties. Clifford good... got...tried... got...of them but...tired of them but they said movie stars have to go to a lot of parties.
Sandy:	What did you do to get this word *tired*?
Karl:	Went on and then I remembered.
Sandy:	That's a great thing to do Karl!

After the short review at the beginning of the session, Karl independently used the strategy, which worked. He also was aware that he used it, as he demonstrated in his answer to the tutor's question. Later in that same session he was reading the sentences *Clifford came home and he's home to stay. He'd rather be with me than in Holly-wood.*

Karl:	Clifford came home and...and...he's home to stay. He...He...He'd right...be...went...with me than in Hollywood. He'd rather be with me than in Hollywood.
Sandy:	That's a great strategy to use. Good job!
Karl:	I think I'm getting used to it.
Sandy:	I'm glad because it helps you so much.

This time the strategy use is independent and the child acknowledges that he is getting used to it.

What this example clearly shows is that children may need coaching when they are learning new strategies. Notice that the coaching involves only very brief comments during reading, with the exception of the brief review at the beginning of the session on July 1. The tutor usually offers the child the opportunity to decide what to do on his own, but when he needs help she suggests the strategy.

Sandy is an artful tutor who used many levels of help. She used *general prompts* such as "What can you do?" She *suggested specific strategies*, "How about if you would skip it?" Sometimes when he used a strategy she *told him what he did*. On several occasions she *did part of the task*. For example, when Karl resisted naming the strategy she said, "skip it and go (pause)" and let Karl finish with "on." Another time she read the beginning of a sentence to get Karl moving, "Because it might make 'blank.'" She also helped Karl know what he knew by *asking him reflective questions*: "What did you do to get this word *tired*?" And by *telling what he did* when he did not answer, "We skipped and came back and it was easy to figure out that word."

Notice that she usually used the prompts in the order of *general* to *specific*. (Chapter 6 of *Variability Not Disability* contains a detailed explanation of the levels of cues.) This order let the child take as much control as possible, but when he could not or did not take control after the general prompt more and more specific help was offered. Notice too, that when the child could not tell what he did, the tutor told the child what he did; eventually the child could tell by himself. This use of prompting at just the level the child needs at a particular time is the way that expert tutors gradually fade their support so that the child learns to do the task independently. The general principle is to use the least amount of help that will allow the child to do the task.

Help children know what they know. The last parts of the process—when the child not only uses the strategy but also names the strategy and knows when he is using it—are very important. Although there is no direct research in tutoring literature, classroom-strategy instruction research shows that strategy use is much more successful when children know the strategies and can verbally describe them. "Knowing what you know" is more formally referred to as metacognitive awareness and knowledge. There is a sound research base demonstrating that metacognitive awareness and knowledge improves strategy use and reading comprehension (Pressley, 1994).

FOR THE SUPERVISOR

I recommend that tutors practice the strategies for getting the children to talk with a peer. Practice with peers helps tutors prepare themselves for children who are reticent and unaccustomed to talking. Because the first tutoring sessions are critical for establishing the relationship between the tutor and the child, and because the tutoring may lose effectiveness if the relationship established is not positive, you should spend ample time in training sessions working on the strategies. (The strategies also are summarized on pages 66–68 of *Variability Not Disability*.)

The information on scaffolding in this chapter may seem overwhelming to tutors. Encourage them to read the section quickly and think of it as a resource to which they can return at various points in their tutoring. At this point, I have used examples to convey the broad concept of strategic scaffolding; I will return to the scaffolding concept in the chapters describing the tutoring activities. Once the tutors are actually tutoring and have mastered basic routines, you may want to return to the scaffolding section of this chapter and also to the strategic scaffolding section of *Variability Not Disability*.

Tutors often have a tendency to prompt at a single level. Basically, when the child encounters a problem, the tutor determines what strategy might work and simply tells the child to do it: "Look at the beginning sound," "Try skipping it," "We can go back and get a running start." Although these may be appropriate prompts some of the time, if all the prompting happens at this level the child may become dependent on the tutor to determine strategies. Movement to more general prompts that give the child more control is very important, but this movement may develop slowly and take as much work and practice as it took for Karl to learn to "skip and come back." You will need to coach the tutors and scaffold their use of prompts strategically.

Chapter 5

~m~

Recording Oral Reading

GOOD TUTORING *requires analyzing children's reading because their oral reading is the major information source for determining how they are reading.* By observing carefully during oral reading, we can learn about the strategies the child uses when encountering problems, and we can learn about how he or she is using letter-sound relations to figure out words. The patterns in oral reading behavior tell us what the child knows and suggest some important strategies or information he or she needs to learn next. Analyzing oral reading also helps us check to make sure the books the child is reading are appropriate. But it is virtually impossible to listen to and remember all the important details of a child's oral reading. Because of the need to analyze children's reading, reading specialists have developed ways of recording oral reading.

SYSTEMS FOR RECORDING ORAL READING

Informal Reading Inventories (IRIs) were the first tools that reading specialists developed to record oral reading. They are sets of passages at various reading levels (first grade, second grade, and third grade, for example) that children read, in order, until they reached a passage that they could not read. A reading specialist recorded each child's performance on these passages in order to learn about the child's reading. Often the IRI results suggested levels at which a child could read by independently (independent level), with instructional support (instructional level), and the first level at which the child could not read (frustration level). Frequently, in addition

73

to these reading levels, the child's error patterns were analyzed to determine his or her strengths and weaknesses. More recently Marie Clay (1993) developed a system called running records (RR) which can be used on the spot to record a child's reading of any passage.

Error Marking Systems

Most oral reading recording systems are similar. They all have marking systems to quickly record anything the reader says that does not match the exact words of the text. Readers can leave out words (omissions), substitute words or nonsense sounds for words (substitutions), and add words that are not in the text (insertions). In addition readers sometimes repeat themselves (repetitions) and sometimes go back and correct themselves (self corrections). Occasionally a child simply will stop and refuse to move on unless you tell the word (defaults).

Table 6 shows the marking systems we use at SRP. They have evolved over the years and have a few peculiarities, but they are the systems we have agreed to use. One of the most important considerations in using an oral-reading recording system is that the people who will be using it agree on its form so that there is consistency among personnel.

For the IRI records, the listener has a copy of the text to mark. When the reader omits a word, the listener circles it; when he or she substitutes a word, the text word is crossed out and the word the reader said is marked above. When the reader adds words, a caret is placed at the point of the addition and the words are written above the line. Repetitions are marked by drawing arrows above the repeated words, and defaults are marked by placing a capital T above them. Self-corrections are noted with a C.

For RR, each correct word is represented by a diagonal stroke. When the child deviates from the text, the examiner writes what the child says above a line and puts what the text words were below the line. An omission is represented with the text word below the line and a dash above the line. A substitution has the child's word above the line and the text's word below the line. An insertion has the child's word above the line and dashes below the line. Repetitions are marked with arrows above the slashes, defaults are indicated with a T, and corrections are marked with a C.

Marking exactly what the child says is the first step in learning from an IRI or RR. What follows is an exercise for you to mark. In the left column is a text; in the

Table 6
Oral Reading Marking Systems

Text: The boy went to the circus.

Omission

Child reads: The boy to the circus.

IRI marking: The boy (went) to the circus.

RR marking: $|| \overline{} \ /// $
went

Substitution

Child reads: The boy want to the circus.

IRI marking: The boy ~~went~~ _want_ to the circus.

RR marking: $|| \dfrac{want}{went} \ ///$

Insertion

Child reads: The boy went right to the circus.

IRI marking: The boy went _right_ ∧ to the circus.

RR marking: $/// |\underline{right}| ///$

Repetition

Child reads: The boy, the boy went to the circus.

IRI marking: The boy ∧ went to the circus.

RR marking: $|/|///$

Self-Correction

Child reads: The boy want, went to the circus.

IRI marking: The boy ~~went~~ _wantC_ to the circus.

RR marking: $|| \dfrac{wantC}{went} \ ///$

Default

Child reads: The boy (long pause) I don't know that word...

Tutor says: went

Child continues: went to the circus

IRI marking: The boy ẘent to the circus.

RR marking: $|| \_T\_ ///$
went

75

right column is what the child read in response to that text. The two columns match line by line.

Text:	Child read:
Jack woke up Saturday morning. He	Jack were up Saturday morning. He
looked out of the window. The ground	looked out of the window. The ground
was white. The trees were white.	was white. The trees were white.
"Oh boy," said Jack, "snow."	"Oh boy," said Jack, "snow."
"What did you say?" asked Tom,	"What did you say?" asked Tom,
rubbing his eyes.	(pause) skip his ears.
"It snowed last night. Get up and	"It snowed last night. Get up and
see," said Jack.	see," said Jack.
Both boys ran to the window.	Both boys ran to the window.
"Look at that!" said Tom. "Come on.	"Look at the!" said Tom. "Come on.
Let's get dressed."	Let's get dressed."
Jack and Tom ran into the kitchen.	Jack and Tom ran into the kitchen.
"Mom!" they said. "It snowed last night.	"Mom!" they said. "It snowed last night.
"Yes," said Mom. "Dad went out to	"Yes," said Mom. "Dad went out to
get your sleds. First we will eat breakfast.	get your skip. First we will eat breakfast.
Then we can have some fun. The first snow	Then we can have some fun. The first snow
is the best!"	is the best!"

Text from *Basic Reading Inventory* (7th Ed.) by Jerry Johns (p. 101). Copyright ©1997 by Kendall/Hunt. Used with permission.

Have someone read the passage as the child read it. First try to mark the reading on the text in the left column using IRI markings. On a second reading, try to write the running record on a blank sheet of paper. Check your markings against the text on page 77.

Several strategies can help you record running records. First, write your markings line by line. When you reach the end of the line in the text, start a new line on your record sheet. Second, when the child reaches the end of a page, draw a horizontal line under the last row of markings for that page. Third, keep your pencil poised on the paper. I make each diagonal stroke (for the correct words) by marking from bottom to top so that if the child deviates from the text I can immediately start writing what the child is saying. Always focus on what the child is saying because you can go back to the text afterward and match what the child said with the text. You cannot go

IRI Markings:	**RR Markings:**
Jack ~~woke~~ *were* up Saturday morning. He	/were / / / / 6 woke
looked out of the window. The ground was	/ / / / / / / / 8
white. The trees were white.	/ / / / / 5
"Oh boy," said Jack, "snow."	/ / / / / 5
"What did you say?" asked Tom,	/ / / / / / 6
(rubbing)/his *ears* ~~eyes~~.	‾‾‾‾‾‾ /ears. 3 rubbing eyes
"It snowed last night. Get up and	/ / / / / / / 7
see," said Jack.	/ / / 3
Both boys ran to the window.	/ / / / / / 6
"Look at ~~that~~ *the*!" said Tom. "Come on.	/ / the / / / / 7 that
Let's get dressed."	/ / / 3
Jack and Tom ran into the kitchen.	/ / / / / / / 7
"Mom!" they said. "It snowed last night."	/ / / / / / / 7
"Yes," said Mom. "Dad went out to	/ / / / / / / 7
get your (sleds) First we will eat breakfast.	/ / skip / / / / / 8 sleds
Then we can have some fun. The first snow	/ / / / / / / / / 9
is the best!"	/ / / 3

back to what the child said unless you tape record—a practice I recommend as you are learning; however, the eventual goal is to do this efficiently and not to have to listen to tapes. Also, remember that it is very easy to begin marking each syllable instead of each word. Be careful that each diagonal mark represents a word.

TOTAL ACCURACY

Marking is the first step in analyzing oral readings and scoring is the next. At SRP we keep two kinds of accuracy scores: Total Accuracy (TA) and Meaningful Accuracy (MA). We begin with TA, which is simply the percentage of text words that the child says correctly on the first try. For ease of explanation, I have taken 100-word passages from an IRI (Johns, 1997). To calculate TA, I count each text word on which the child made an error. I subtract the number of errors from the total number of words and then divide that result by the total number of words to convert it to a percentage. I do not count repetitions as errors. In the reading shown earlier, the child made five errors: (1) *were/woke*, (2) ———/*rubbing*, (3) *ears/eyes*, (4) *the/that*, and (5) *skip/sleds*. There were 100 words in the passage and the child said 100 minus 5, or 95 words correctly on the first try. To convert this to a percentage of the total words (in this case 100) we divide by 100. The TA score is 95%. At SRP a TA score of 95% suggests that the child is reading the passage at an independent level.

We follow the reading with a retelling to see if the child understood the story. The child who read this passage knew that the two boys woke and saw snow and that when they went downstairs to eat breakfast Mother told them that Dad had gone out to get their sleds. The child understood the passage. Note that the child knew that Dad was getting the sleds even though he never read *sleds* out loud. It is safe to assume that the child read this passage at an independent level. The following exercise is the transcription of the same child reading another passage.

Text:	Child read:
One day Spotty went for a walk. The sun was warm. Spotty walked to the pond. There he saw a frog. The frog was on a log. Spotty wanted to play. Spotty began to	One day one day Spotty went for a walk. The sun was warm. So skip walked to the pond. There he saw a frog. A frog was on a long. Spotty until to play. Spotty become began to
bark. The frog just sat there. Spotty jumped into the water. The frog jumped in too. Spotty did not know what to do. The water was very deep. It went way over his head. Spotty moved his legs. Soon his head came out of the water. He kept on moving. He came to the	dart for. The frog just sat there. Spotty jumped into the water. The frog jumped into. Spotty did not know what to do. The water was very deep. It went way over he said. Spotty moved Let he let soo be head come out of the water. He kept on moving. He came to the

other side of the pond. That is how Spotty learned to swim.

outer side of the pond. That is how Spotty learned to swim.

Once again, this is a 100-word passage and if we look at the scoring the child has made 17 errors or has a TA score of (100 minus 17)/ 100 or 83% which indicates that the passage is too difficult or at a frustration level. Look at the difference in the readings of the two passages. In the first passage we have the sense that the child is understanding the story. In the second passage, the child is making so many errors that it is clear he is not understanding. Table 7 summarizes the errors.

On retelling the child clearly did not understand that Spotty did not know how to swim and learned because he jumped in the pond to chase the frog. This is the

IRI Markings:

One day Spotty went for a walk. The

sun was warm. ~~Spotty~~ *So* walked to the pond.

There he saw a frog. ~~The~~ *A* frog was on a

~~log~~ *long*. Spotty ~~wanted~~ *until* to play. Spotty ~~began~~ *become*c to

~~bark~~ *dart for*. The frog just sat there.

Spotty jumped into the water. The

frog jumped ~~in too~~ *into*. Spotty did not know

what to do. The water was very deep.

It went way over ~~his head~~ *he said*. Spotty moved

~~his legs~~ *Let he let so be come*. Soon ~~his~~ head ~~came~~ out of the

water. He kept on moving. He came to the

~~other~~ *outer* side of the pond. That is how Spotty

learned to swim.

RR Markings:

/ / / / / / / / [8]

/ / / So skip / / / / [8]
spotty

/ / / / / A / / / / [10]
the

~~long~~ / until / / / become / [8]
log wanted began

dart for. / / / / / [6]
bark

/ / / / / / [6]

/ / into ——— / / / / [8]
in too

/ / / / / / / / [8]

/ / / / he said / / [8]
hishead

Let he let soo be / come / / / [9]
his legs soon his came

/ / / / / / / / / [9]

outer / / / / / / / / [9]
other

/ / / [3]

difference between independent- and frustration-level reading. For total accuracy we use the cutoffs in Table 8 to estimate reading levels. Children should be encouraged to read material at their independent and instructional reading levels. If they constantly read frustration-level material (and at school many children are forced to read frustration-level materials), they will not get much out of their reading except bad habits. Recording children's oral reading is useful because it teaches us to recognize these levels. Often we are so concerned about the child keeping up that we are satisfied with frustration-level reading. We should not be.

Meaningful Accuracy

Notice that although the child corrected *began* without help from the teacher, I counted it as an error in the TA score. The TA score represents the percentage of text words with which the child had difficulty on the first try, and because the child initially had difficulty with *began*, I counted it as an error. I also calculate an MA

Table 7	
Error Summary for Spotty Passage	
———	Spotty
A	the
long	log
until	wanted
become	began
dart	bark
for	———
into	in
———	too
he	his
said	head
he	his
let	legs
soo	Soon
be	his
come	came
outer	other

Table 8		
Reading Levels for Total Accuracy		
95–100	independent	
90–94	instructional	
below 89	frustration	

score, and in this score I count only errors that change the basic meaning of the passage. Because an error that is corrected does not affect meaning, I do not count self-corrections as errors in the MA score. This method of scoring gives me maximally different information from the two scores. The TA is merely a representation of the child's accuracy in basic decoding. The MA score is a representation of the child's access to the meaning of the passage through decoding. The following exercise demonstrates the usefulness of the MA Score.

Text:

"See the small birds," said Jim.
"They are looking in the snow. They want

food."
"The snow is deep," said Meg. "They

cannot find food."

Jim said, "Let's help them."
"Yes," said Meg. We can get bread

for them."
Jim and Meg ran home. They asked
Mother for bread. Mother gave bread to
them. Then they ran to find the birds.
"There are the birds," said Meg.
"Give them the bread."
Jim put the bread on the snow.

Child read:

"See the small birds," said Jim.
"They are looking in the show. They went
they want
food."
"They show. The show is deep," said Meg.
uh   "They
uh cannot find any can't find cannot find
food."

Jim said, "Let's help them."
"Yes," said Meg. We can help the we can
help get bread
for them."
Jim and Meg went and ran home. They asked
Mother for bread. Mother gave bread to
them. Then they ran to find the birds.
"They are they are the birds," said Meg.
"Give them some bread."
Jim put some bread on on on the um ground
would make sense...

Meg said, "Look at the birds! They are eating the bread."
"They are happy now," said Jim.
"They are fat and happy."

Said Meg, "Look at the birds! They are eating the bread."
"They are happy now," said Jim.
"They are fat and happy."

Text from *Basic Reading Inventory* (7th Ed.) by Jerry Johns (p. 165). Copyright ©1997 by Kendall/Hunt. Used with permission.

IRI Markings:

"See the small birds," said Jim.

"They are looking in the ~~snow~~ *show* They ~~want~~ *went* c

food."

"~~The snow~~ *They show* is deep," said Meg. "~~They~~ *uh*
cannot
can't ^*any* c
cannot find food."

Jim said, "Let's help them."

"Yes," said Meg. We can get bread *help the* c

for them."

Jim and Meg ^*went and* ran home. They asked

Mother for bread. Mother gave bread to

them. Then they ran to find the birds.

"~~There~~ *They* are the birds," said Meg.

"Give them ~~the~~ *some* bread."

Jim put the bread on the ~~snow~~ *ground*.

~~Meg said~~, *Said Meg* "Look at the birds! They

are eating the bread."

"They are happy now," said Jim.

"They are fat and happy."

RR Markings:

/ / / / / / 6

" / / / / / show. / went 8 c
      Snow want
/ 1

"They show. / / / / . uh / 7
the snow
/ / any / 3 c

/ / / / / 5

/ / / / / help the / /

/ / 2

/ / / went and / / / / 7

/ / / / / / / 7

/ / / / / / / / 8

They / / / / / 6
There
/ / some / 4
the
/ / / / / / um ground 7
Snow
Said Meg, / / / / / 7
meg said
/ / / / 4

/ / / / / / 6

/ / / / / 5

I always begin scoring by calculating a TA score. By mechanically identifying all the text words on which there were errors, I start out with a baseline that is easy to replicate. Because the tutor does not have to make decisions about what kind of error the child is making, it is easier to get agreement among various personnel on the TA score. There are not many judgment calls in TA scoring because it is simply the percentage of text words pronounced correctly on the first try. There were 14 errors for a TA score of 86%. On the basis of TA we would decide that this was a frustration-level passage. However, in the third column of the error list (see Table 7 on page 80), I note self-corrections with an SC, errors that do not change the author's intended meaning of the passage with an MS (for makes sense), and errors that do change the intended meaning of the passage with an NS (no sense). In calculating MA only NS errors count.

In this case there are 4 no sense errors so the MA score is 96%. According to guidelines for MA (see Table 9) the passage is instructional level for this child. The chart summarizes these levels for TA and MA. In this case the child's reading was fairly fluent and she was clearly following the meaning of the passage when she said, "um ground would make sense." Her retelling also indicated that she understood that the birds were hungry and that the children were feeding them. She had difficulty with one key word, *snow*, which appeared three times, but overall she was reading and understanding the passage.

The MA score gives a better picture of how the child is decoding in relation to understanding the story and thus is usually a better indicator of reading level. However, when there are large discrepancies between TA and MA this is a sign that there may be some decoding issues—either a lack of an adequate sight vocabulary or inadequate knowledge or use of letter-sound relations.

Table 9
Oral Reading Accuracy Levels

Level	TA	MA
independent	95–100	98–100
instructional	90–94	95–97
frustration	below 90	below 95

ERROR PATTERNS

Oral reading analysis can be very helpful in deciding whether a child is reading appropriate-level text. IRIs, particularly those that are keyed to instructional materials such as IRIs that accompany many reading series, can help you decide where to place children in sequenced reading materials. Running records, which can be used easily with any material that a child is reading, can help you determine if children are making good choices in their independent reading. However, oral reading recording systems also can provide important information about how a child, particularly a beginning reader, is applying word-identification strategies. For example, let us compare the errors the child who read the "Spotty" passage made with the errors of the child who read the "Small Birds" passage (see Table 10). Remember both were reading at frustration-level based on the TA score.

Table 10
Error Comparison for Spotty and Small Birds Passages

	Spotty				Small Birds		
1.	——————	Spotty	NS	1.	show	snow	NS
2.	A	the	MS	2.	went	want	SC
3.	long	log	NS	3.	They	The	SC
4.	until	wanted	NS	4.	show	snow	NS
5.	become	began	SC	5.	uh	——	MS
6.	dart	bark	NS	6.	any	——	MS
7.	for	——————	NS	7.	help the	——————	MS/SC
8.	into	in	NS	8.	went and	——————	MS
9.	——————	too	NS	9.	They	There	NS
10.	he	his	NS	10.	some	the	MS
11.	said	head	NS	11.	some	the	MS
12.	he	his	NS	12.	ground	snow	NS
13.	let	legs	NS	13.	said	Meg	MS
14.	soo	Soon	NS	14.	Meg	said	MS
15.	be	his	NS				
16.	come	came	NS				
17.	outer	other	NS				

The most striking difference is in the number of NS errors. The first child seemed to make many NS errors and did not return to correct them. The second child made many more errors that preserved the author's intended meaning. It may be that the text was simply too difficult for the first child and he could not use meaning to monitor his reading. The second child, although reading at a similar TA level, was using meaning to monitor because many of her errors *did* preserve the author's meaning.

A second feature of the two lists is that they differ, at least for some key errors, in whether or not they preserve the graphic or the meaningful aspects of the text. In the first list the NS errors usually have some graphic similarity to the text word. Usually the initial consonant is preserved and sometimes the word is graphically quite close, for example, *outer/other*. The second child seemed less restricted by the print, often inserting words that fit with the flow of language and made sense, venturing for example, *ground* for *snow* after deciding that *show* (visually closer) did not make sense.

You can analyze oral error patterns to determine if the child is paying attention to beginnings, middles, and ends of words; to see if there are consistent errors with particular sounds or classes of sounds such as vowels; to see if she is consistently missing or confusing particular words with each other; and to evaluate her strategies for word identification—does she simply skip unknown words, or does she reread and read on and return when she has difficulty. When children have become fairly fluent and mastered basic word identification oral reading records become less informative. Once decoding is mastered our record-keeping system must emphasize silent reading comprehension. At that point we switch to the techniques explained in Chapter 7.

FOR THE SUPERVISOR

Marking IRIs and taking Running Records is the first step in keeping track of children's reading. It is not as easy at looks on paper. It takes many practice runs to become accurate, and when I teach tutors to record oral reading I routinely let them listen to a tape three times—once as they watch me mark the reading, once as they try to mark, and at least once more as they try again. They look at me in disbelief when I tell them that within a few weeks they will be able to record oral reading quite efficiently. (I do not say effortlessly because it always requires careful attention.) A student recently declared that real teachers could not possibly do this and the only reason that I could was that I had memorized the tape. (I was very familiar with the tape.) Fortunately, several practicing teachers who use RR talked with the class and showed their running records.

Another issue in recording oral reading is disagreements over what the child actually said. Because we often are working from tapes in class exercises, there are times when what the child says is not clear. These disagreements can quickly confuse the class if you allow them to become the focus of attention. The way I handle this issue is to acknowledge from the beginning that we will not always agree. I point out that our scoring on individual errors may vary, but even if we do not agree exactly on every error, we usually agree on the overall level. I also point out that I would never make critical instructional decisions on the basis of a single IRI or Running Record. In tutoring we have many opportunities to take running records and to check on reading levels, so disagreements on isolated errors are not very important in the long run. What is important is that we learn to record children's reading and analyze it regularly so that it can help inform our teaching.

Chapter 6

Learning From Children's Writing

READING AND *writing are closely related to each other; I often think of reading as receiving messages and writing as sending or composing messages.* Because of these shared aspects, we can use children's writing to learn about their knowledge of both reading and writing. In this chapter I examine several samples of children's writing and as I look at each one, I emphasize how it shows what the child knows and what possible next steps in reading and writing it suggests for the child. Although I would never make a decision about where to go next in literacy learning on the basis of a single writing sample, each sample is useful to present possibilities that can be explored and confirmed through further observation of the child's reading and writing performance.

In order to understand the analysis of these samples you may want to refer to Chapter 3, because analyzing writing samples is dependent on knowledge of writing development. You cannot determine what the child knows or decide what comes next without understanding writing development. After presenting the examples, I provide an outline for evaluating writing samples that we have developed over the years as we have tried to help students learn to write (Fielding, Hammons, & Janson, 1991).

EMERGENT READERS

Peter, a fourth-grade child, wrote the story in Figure 12. When asked to read the story he read the following:

The Chocolate Bear

Once a chocolate bear was walking through the forest. A hunter shot it. The hunter went over to the bear and laid his hand. Then he lifted it and said, "This is a chocolate bear." Then he took it to a museum and said, "I have a chocolate bear. If you put it in a cold spot you can have it." Then everyone in the whole world saw it.

When looking at a writing sample like this, our tendency is to be appalled. How can a child entering fourth grade write so poorly? This, however, is the wrong question. The appropriate questions are: What does this child know about reading and writing? and What are the next important steps to take in literacy learning? Before you continue reading, write down at least five things that Peter knows about reading and writing that you can identify from this sample.

Peter actually knows quite a lot. He gave his story a title and his reading of the story suggests his understanding that a story must fit a certain pattern—that it has an introduction ("once there was a chocolate bear"); that it must have characters (the hunter and the bear); that there must be a problem (the hunter shot the chocolate bear); and that the problem must be resolved (the bear was displayed in a museum). The sample also indicates some knowledge of the world; because the bear is chocolate, it needs to be displayed in a cool place, and museums are places for displays.

In addition to story and world knowledge, Peter also displayed significant knowledge of the writing system. He spelled the common sight words, *the, he, I, can,* and *see,* correctly. He wrote from left to right, leaving spaces between words. Although it is difficult to match the sample word by word to the story as Peter read it, it is clear that *bell* represents *bear* consistently throughout the story. His representation thus uses the correct beginning sound. He also included vowels in appropriate positions in each of his invented spellings.

A natural first objective for Peter would be to begin to match spoken words to written words. I also might consider reinforcing and extending his use of correct beginning letters and sounds, and if this were easily accomplished work next on the inclusion of correct ending sounds and letters.

The second sample (see Figure 13, on page 90) is from a first-grade child who is further along in the emergent period. It reads, *My name is Andy. I have one brother. I*

Figure 12
Peter's Writing Sample

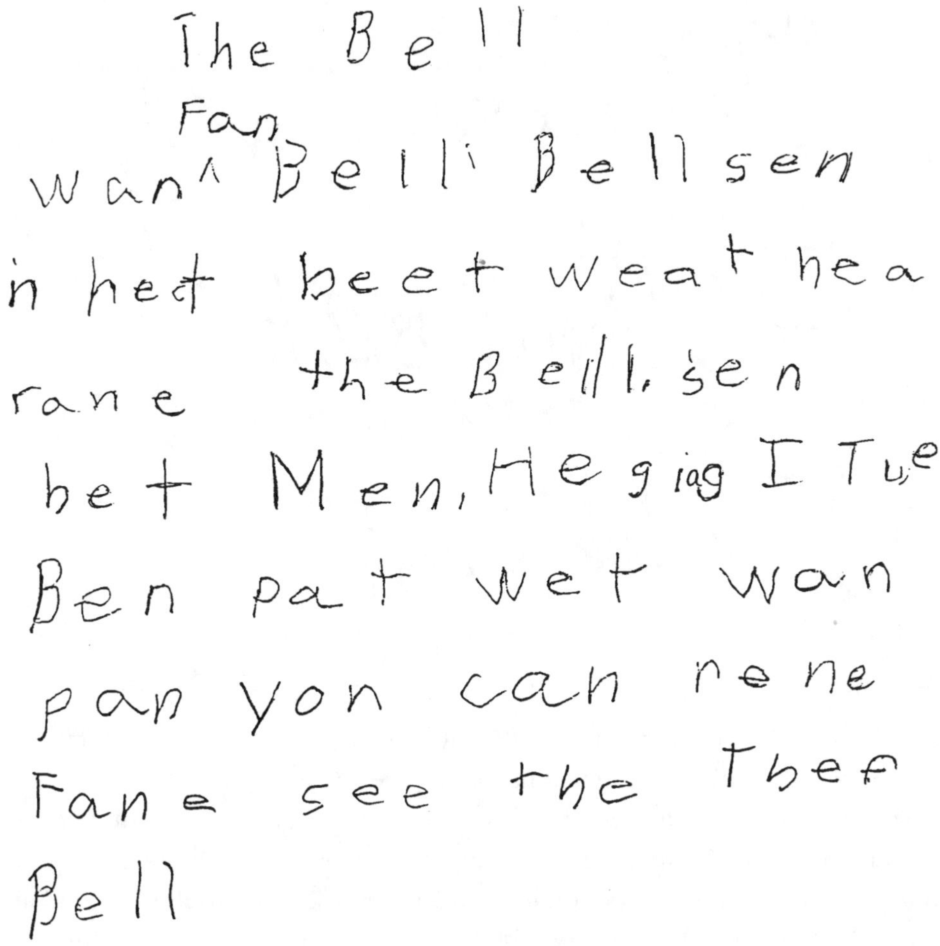

The Bell
                Fan
Wan Belli Bell sen
n het beet weat hea
rane the Bell, sen
het Men, He giag I Tue
Ben pat wet wan
pan yon can rene
Fane see the Thef
Bell

like math. It was written as an introductory note to a potential tutor. Before you continue reading, list four or five things that Andy knows about writing.

Andy understood the demands of the task and told the tutor important information about himself. There were 10 words in his message and he spelled three correctly (*is*, *I* written correctly twice, and his name). His other spellings are phonetic and reflect his speech—*nam* includes appropriate letters to represent the three sounds of

---

Figure 13
Andy's Writing Sample

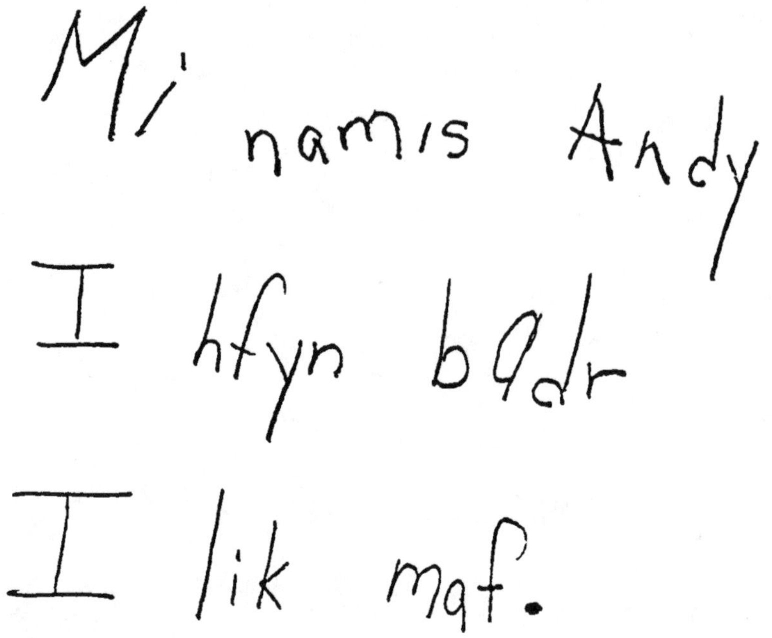

Mi namis Andy

I hfyn badr

I lik maf.

---

name as do *lik* for *like* and *maf* for *math* (Andy pronounced *math* as /maf/). *Hf* for *have* included a correct initial and final consonant, given Andy's pronunciation of *have* as /haf/. *Yn* for *one* uses *y* to represent the /w/ sound heard at the beginning of *one* and he correctly supplied the final *n*. His spelling of *badr* for *brother*, although it omits the *r* of the beginning *br-* blend, does include an *a* to represent a vowel sound and an *r* to represent the final *-er*. The *d* in the middle is consistent with Andy's pronunciation of "brother" as /brudr/.

Andy understood that words and print must match and he also understood that written English follows an alphabetic principal, that the letters in written words stand for the sounds heard in spoken words. In most cases he correctly represented the sound he heard with an appropriate letter. In one place where he used an inappropriate letter, *y* to represent the /w/ sound of *one*, he used a plausible letter, as the name of the letter *y* does begin with the /w/ sound. He had a good understanding of consonant sounds, used appropriate representations for long vowels (*a* in *name* and *i* in *my*), and also knew that vowels are in words like *brother* and *math*. He was at the phonetic stage of invented spelling and could be expected to apply his knowledge of the alphabetic principle and word-to-print matching in his reading. Possible goals for Andy include expanding his sight vocabulary and helping him make the transition to the visual stages of spelling development.

BEGINNING READERS

Heidi wrote the captions for three pages of a wordless picture book (Figure 14) during a screening session for SRP. She read the following captions:

1. He gets a frog.
2. There are four of us.
3. Go away big frog.

Before you continue reading, make a list of what Heidi knows about writing.

Heidi's captions are consistent with the illustrations in the book and she seemed to interpret the task as telling what the characters were doing or saying. She wrote 13 words, 10 of which were spelled correctly. Her misspellings, *fong* for *frog* and *or way* for *away*, are reasonable and readable representations. She used a consistent spelling for *frog* that has beginning and final letters correct. She spelled the second syllable of *away* correctly and used a vowel and *r* to represent the vowel sound of the first syllable.

Heidi was developing a sight vocabulary. She knew how to spell a number of high-frequency vocabulary words (*he, gets, a, there, are, four, of, us, go, way,* and *big*). Her misspellings indicate knowledge of beginning and ending letter and sounds and

---

Figure 14
Heidi's Writing Sample

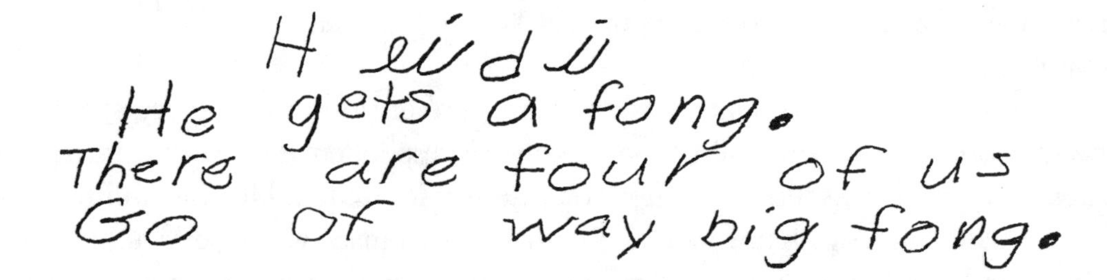

Heidi

He gets a fong.
There are four of us
Go of way big fong.

---

an ability to hear syllables (as in *away*). I suspect that Heidi may have been restricted in her writing by her spelling, and that she wrote short sentences and stuck to words that she knew how to spell wherever possible. One goal for Heidi might be to encourage her to expand her writing to include more of her thoughts. Continued expansion of sight vocabulary and development in spelling also would be possible goals.

Billy, who in Figure 15 was responding to a letter from his tutor, was in third grade. Write down some of the things Billy knows about reading and writing before you continue reading.

The content is appropriate to a letter of introduction. He told the recipient that he liked a story she wrote and that he would write one in return. He gave background information on where he lived and used to live, he named his brother and sisters, and said he likes to play sports. He concluded by asking for similar information about the recipient and by fulfilling his opening promise to send something.

Billy's letter reads:

> Dear Mr. XXXXX,
>
> I like your story you wrote to me. I am going to write you a story. I like Waterloo. I used to live in Chicago. I've got two brothers and sisters—Mark, Serina, and Tamara. I like to play sports. What are your sisters' and brothers' names? What do you look like? I am going to draw you a picture of a dog.

Billy's letter has 62 words, 39 of which are spelled correctly. Many of his correctly spelled words are common sight vocabulary (for example, *I*, *your*, *to*, *and*, *going*, *you*, *a*, and *look*). He also was successful with *brothers* and *sisters*. Of the 23 words that he spelled phonetically, most contain correct beginning and ending letters—*rt* and *rit* for *write*, *fin* for *fine*, *liev* for *live*. Billy used his visual memory to remember spellings. For example, the words *liev* for *live*, *paly* for *play*, *naem* for *name*, and *waht* for *what* contain all the letters of the words including silent letters such as *e* in *live* and *name*, *y* in *play*, and the *a* in *what*, which is pronounced as short *u*. Billy was in a transitional spelling stage in which he understood the letters and sounds and was beginning to rely on visual memory for correct spellings. Often in his visual spellings the letters are out of order.

Billy had control of many basic writing conventions. He allowed space between most words. There is also a one-to-one correspondence between printed and spoken words. Billy's letters are not consistently formed and legible and he may have had difficulties with fine motor coordination that made writing difficult for him. However, he understood that letters open with a salutation and his content is ap-

Figure 15
Billy's Writing Sample

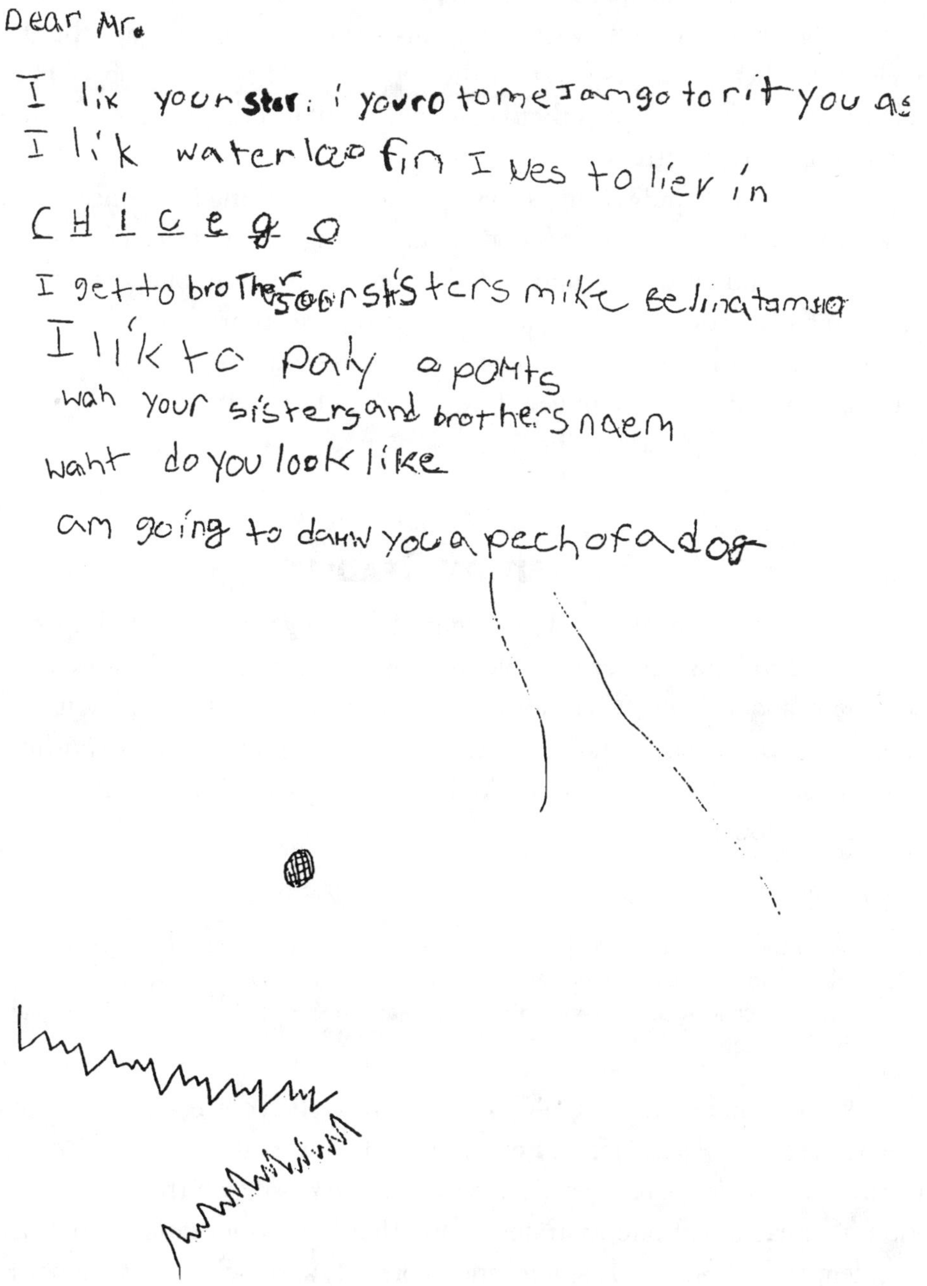

Dear Mr.

I lik your star, i youro tome Jamgo to rit you as
I lik waterloo fin I ves to lier in
CHICEGO
I getto brother sogrsisters mike Belinatamsa
I llik ta paly apomts
wah your sisters and brothers naem
waht do you look like

am going to dahw you a pech of a dog

propriate to the letter form. He did not use a closing or a signature but he may have thought of the picture as a closing.

Billy consistently and appropriately capitalized the word *I*. He was inconsistent in capitalizing names, doing so with two of his siblings' names but not the third. It is not clear whether he understood that the beginnings of sentences should be capitalized because all the sentences that begin with capitals begin with the word *I*. He also did not use end punctuation.

Although Billy's handwriting is awkward and his spelling is inconsistent, there was much that he knew and understood about reading and writing. We might work with Billy to expand his writing and include more information. Support for his writing that emphasizes content might help him begin to see himself as a writer. Another issue to explore is his visual memory for common sight words in both his reading and writing. Some help in spelling and work with sight words might help him move forward in both reading and writing.

TRANSITION READERS

Mary wrote the kangaroo story in Figure 16 during writing workshop. She was very interested in kangaroos, read several books about them, and wanted to write her own book about them. What does Mary know about reading and writing? This was a first draft of her book and in it she was clearly attempting an expository format and chose to include facts about kangaroos that were interesting to her. Her story reads as follows:

Kangaroos

After the sun goes down, the kangaroos go and find food. Kangaroos live in mobs. The oldest kangaroo leads a mob. Wild dogs hunt kangaroos. Kangaroos do not run. They hop on the back legs. Before giving birth, she cleans the pouch. For six months the baby stays in the pouch.

The story includes 52 words, 46 of which are spelled correctly. Mary may have used her reference books to support her spelling. Her misspellings—*afat* for *after*, *bowe* for *down*, *odlist* for *oldest*, *mod* for *mob*, and *says* for *stays*—suggest that she used a combination of visual and phonetic strategies and that letter orientation and order may be a problem for her. She used capitalization correctly and included end punctuation, although she used it inappropriately in her opening sentence. The sample indicates that Mary had a sophisticated understanding of English literacy and understood the style of informational prose. One area for growth might be organization, because she listed the facts randomly and thus may need help in transforming the information from other sources for use in her own prose.

Figure 16
Mary's Writing Sample

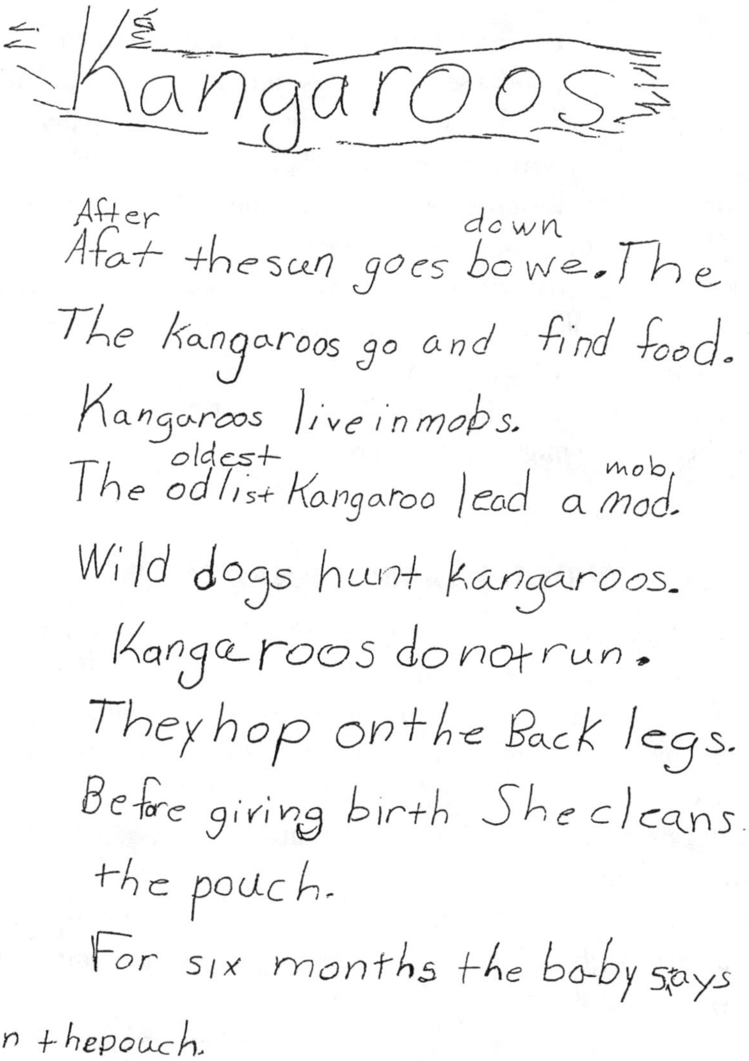

Kangaroos

After
Afat the sun goes bowe (down). The
The kangaroos go and find food.
Kangaroos live in mobs.
The odlist (oldest) kangaroo lead a mod (mob).
Wild dogs hunt kangaroos.
Kangaroos do not run.
They hop on the Back legs.
Before giving birth She cleans
the pouch.
For six months the baby says
in the pouch.

Karen wrote the final sample (Figure 17) on a day when the air conditioner broke and the class had their writing workshop outside. It reads as follows on the next page.

> The sun is bright and warm and the birds are coming and going. People walk from here to there. The trees are green and the ground has green grass and yellow and red and other colors of flowers growing too. Now is when animals look for food and people work. And cars go by and little ants move around and birds find them and take them back to their babies. One bird flew up right beside me and he was a boy bird. And then a girl bird flew up right beside him and they flew away. Now about the ants. One of them crawled on my leg. And I had fun writing this story but I have to go. So see you later.

Before reading on, decide what Karen knows about reading and writing.

Karen wrote in the genre of descriptive prose and it is clear that she had a sophisticated understanding of it. Notice the inclusion of a series of pairs in the opening lines that give the piece a sort of repetitive and poetic rhythm. She also was struggling with the notion of transitions, (*Now about the ants…*), endings, and audience (*see you later*). These may be possible growth areas.

She had developed a fairly extensive sight vocabulary, spelling words such as *the, sun, is, and, came, people, walk, from, are, grass,* and *now* correctly. It is also clear that she was experimenting with different ways of representing long vowel sounds— *brite, green, grean, rite, beside, besid, riteing*. Building on this experimentation in all her reading and her writing might be appropriate.

WRITING SAMPLE ANALYSIS

Pieces of writing a child does on his or her own before revision or editing and without an adult telling him or her how to spell words correctly can be very useful for understanding a child's stage of literacy development and planning appropriate instruction. When analyzed carefully, these samples provide information about the child's knowledge of the functions and purposes of writing, writing conventions, letter-sound relations, phonics, spelling, capitalization and punctuation rules, sight words, expository and narrative text structures, sequencing, and book language. The key to using a child's writing to find out what he or she knows is to look at it before it has gone through the revision or editing process *with someone else*. You need to know what the child can do without help.

You may be tempted to notice only what the child does wrong in his or her writing, and you need to avoid this temptation. There are many things that every child

Figure 17
Karen's Writing Sample

The sun is brite ond whorm and the
bards ared came and goring people walk
from hear to thare The trees are green
and the giond hase grean grass ard yello and
Ted and outh coulers of folws growingtow,
Now is when almes look fore food and
people wark.
And car go bay and liatts Ants
move a rown and bards find them and
tack them to thary badys one bard
flow up rite be side me and it was
a dou dird and then a girl
  flow up rite be sid him and
thay flow a way. Now a bot the
Ants onw of them corld on
nag lage and I had fun riteing
this story but I haft to go sows
fou larty.

Table 11
Things You May Learn From a Child's Unaided Writing

Narrative and Expository Conventions

     a. Is content appropriate and well developed?

     b. Does the child use story conventions such as "Once upon a time" or "Happily ever after"?

     c. Does the plot or organization seem to be based in part on a well-known book or story?

     d. Do the events in stories build to a climax?

     e. In expository writing, is the main point of the writing clear?

     f. Is the organization or sequence of events easy to follow?

Style

     a. Is the style conversational or literary? Does it resemble an essay?

     b. Do you notice any features like descriptive language, use of dialogue, or use of repetition?

     c. Does he or she use language typically found in books more than in conversation (For example, "meanwhile" or "I'm sorry to say")?

Writing Conventions

     a. Are there spaces between words?

     b. Does the writing go from left to right?

     c. Does the writing go from the top of the page to the bottom?

     d. Are paragraphs indented?

Punctuation and Capitalization Conventions

     a. Is there end punctuation?

     b. Are commas used?

     c. Are names and beginnings of sentences capitalized?

     d. Is punctuation used to indicate how the writing should be read (for example, an exclamation point to indicate excitement)?

     e. Is dialogue set off with quotation marks? Are book titles underlined?

(continued)

does right. Notice these things first. Then you should look for errors that indicate knowledge—a spelling, phonics, or punctuation rule that has been used but in an inappropriate place, or a letter that indicates a correct sound but the wrong choice of spelling. Then you should look for signs that the child is on the brink of learning

---

Table 11
Things You May Learn From a Child's Unaided Writing (continued)

Phonics Knowledge

    a. Which sounds are represented appropriately: Initial consonants, most consonants, vowels?

    b. Is there a letter to represent all or most *sounds* in a word? If not, then which sounds have a letter (for example, initial or final consonants only)?

    c. When spellings are not conventional, do the letters represent an alternative way to spell the sound (for example, spelling *crack* as *krack* or *done* as *dun*)? Do they represent the way the child says the word (for example, *with* as *wif*)? Do they indicate that the child is remembering letters that he or she has seen (*paly* for *play*)?

    d. Even when spellings are not correct, do they represent any of the most common phonics generalizations? Which ones? (For example, spelling *dream* as *dreme* suggests that the child knows the "long vowel, silent *e*" rule.)

---

something new, for example, spelling a word several different ways in one piece as if trying to decide which way looks the best. *Then* you might point out one or two things the child does not yet seem to know. If you only look for what the child has done wrong or only interpret errors as signs of what the child does not know, you will miss much of what the writing sample has to tell you.

Table 11 lists some questions that can guide your analyses. These questions should not be interpreted as a definitive list. Depending on the child's writing maturity you are likely to notice some things more than others. You certainly may notice things that are not on the list. Be sure that you always begin your analyses by responding to the content of the writing.

FOR THE SUPERVISOR

One of the biggest challenges in getting tutors to use children's writing to inform their teaching is getting past the "correction" mentality. Tutors often have learned to read and write in traditional "red pencil" settings. They have a tendency to emphasize correctness in spelling and mechanics such as grammar and punctuation over content. One thing I emphasize is that tutors always comment about the content of the writing first whether they are talking to the child author or about the child author. This helps to keep the focus of literacy instruction where it should be—on meaning.

I also insist that tutors always tell me what the child knows before talking about what the child does not know. This is particularly difficult for tutors who work with struggling readers whose literacy development lags far behind their physical and emotional development. It is often the contrast in these developmental levels that captures the tutors' (and probably everyone elses') attention. However, I find that if I insist on identifying what the child knows and can do, the tutors begin to see beyond the developmental gap.

Finally, I make sure the tutors do not detail everything the child does not know. Instead I ask them to focus on what the child needs to learn next. Tutors must ask themselves what is the most important next step that we should focus on next? What will help move this child forward? Writing sample analysis, when done with focus on what the child knows and what the child might learn next, can provide important information to the tutor. The careful analysis of writing also can help create the habit of analysis with focus on strengths and on what comes next in all that the tutor does.

Chapter 7

Assessing Comprehension

THERE ARE *many ways to learn about a child's reading comprehension.* Having children read passages and answer questions about what they have read is the most commonly used method of assessment. Typically, children read a short (200 to 300 words) passage and are asked between 5 and 10 questions that usually include literal-level, main-idea, and inferential-level questions, and sometimes a question about vocabulary meaning. A score of 70% usually is considered adequate for instructional-level material.

Comprehension assessment is very important because comprehension is the essence of reading. If we "read" something and have not understood it, we have not really read it. As I noted above, comprehension is usually assessed with questions. Because this is the assessment strategy most often used in schools, most tutors will be familiar with it. This chapter will focus on three other methods of assessment—think-alouds, summarizing, and retelling.

THINK-ALOUDS FOR ASSESSMENT

Think-alouds are just what the name implies—the reader stops at predetermined points during her reading to think out loud about what she is reading. Although this technique is unfamiliar to many new tutors, it can be quite useful because it gives us some idea of the processes children are using to understand the texts they read. To further explain I will refer to an exercise I did with some older children. They each read the paragraphs presented in Figure 18. On the copy that students read, there was a red slash after each sentence or main clause. I told students to stop at the red slashes and, "Tell me what it means, tell me what you are thinking."

The biggest difference I saw in good and poor readers was that good readers talked about why the author was telling them information and what it meant. They often used their own words to explain what they were thinking and they connected information across sentences. Struggling readers simply repeated back the words of the sentence and did not seem to be making much sense of their reading (Wilson & Hammill, 1982). Figure 19 contains two readers' responses to selected phrases.

Student A scored at the 25th percentile on a standardized reading comprehension test and Student B scored at the 99th percentile. In items 1, 2, and 6, Student A simply repeated words from the sentence. In items 3, 4, and 5, Student A seemed to be doing some interpreting, though it is still within sentences, and is often confused. In clause 3 he seemed puzzled by the term *populous*, and in clause 7 it is clear that he focused on the United States rather than Java. He also interpreted "not habitable" as a positive term in item 5.

Figure 18
School Text Excerpt on Indonesia

About two-thirds of the people of Indonesia live on the island of Java, the political heart of the country. Java is about as large as the state of New York, but sixty million people live there. New York has less than twenty million, yet we think of it as a very populous state. If the Javanese were spread evenly over their island, there would be more than 1,000 on each square mile. But by no means is every square mile of Java habitable. There are many mountains, including more than 100 volcanoes, seventeen of which are active.

It is remarkable that the land of Java has been made to support so many people. Natural conditions are responsible in part. Rains falling on the volcanic mountains wash fresh soil down to the lowlands. The warm climate is favorable for the growth of rice. Since rice is usually grown in flooded fields, it is safe from all but the severest droughts. In yield per acre rice is hard to beat.

Dutch rule also aided population growth. Local wars were stopped. Improved farming methods were introduced. Hygiene was somewhat improved. Railroads and highways helped trade and the flow of food. All this permitted more people to survive.

Jones, S.B., & Murphy, M.F. (1976). *Geography and World Affairs*. Chicago, IL: Rand McNally.

Figure 19
Two Students' Responses to Selected Clauses

---

1. Java is about as large as the state of New York
    A. New York's just as large at that state.
    B. It gives me an idea of how big it is.

2. But sixty million people live there.
    A. They live in...Indonesia...about 60 people live.
    B. So it's well populated.

3. Yet we think of it as a very populous state.
    A. It means it's very popular to us as a state.
    B. That's just what Americans think; that doesn't mean much.

4. If the Javanese were spread evenly over their island there would be more than one thousand on each square mile.
    A. They...if you spread families out all over...if you spread person...everybody out over the United States there'd be on per 1,000 mile.
    B. That just shows how many people there are again.

5. But by no means is every square mile of Java habitable.
    A. Means that in Java the islands, islands are good or whatever.
    B. So there's probably centers of population that are...that there mostly people live.

6. Natural conditions are responsible in part.
    A. What conditions are part.
    B. Nature is partly responsible for Java being able to support so many people.

Student B on the other hand went beyond each sentence to gain an understanding of the author's overall message. In items 1, 3, and 4 he commented on the author's purpose in giving the information, and in items 2 and 5 he drew conclusions not directly stated in the text. His response to item 6 shows that he clearly integrated information across sentences because he understood what the natural conditions do.

Student's think-alouds also can help us understand what is going wrong in their comprehension more specifically. Figure 20 again gives selected clauses and students' responses to them.

Figure 20
Students' Responses Reveal Specific
Comprehension Difficulties

---

1. Yet we think of it as a populous state.

   Cause it's a fascinating place to see.

2. Hygiene was somewhat improved.

   I don't know what hygiene is. Is that like, oh what is it you put on the crops and doesn't it keep the weeds from coming up?

3. Since rice is usually grown in flooded fields, it is safe from all but the severest droughts.

   They can still raise rice even though there's lots of floods.

4. It is remarkable that the land of Java has been made to support so many people.

   What conditions are part.

5. Dutch rule aided population growth.

   It means more of the people went by the pop…rules, so they live better.

In item 1 the student probably was confused about *populous*. She may have actually read the word as *popular* or, if she read it as *populous*, was confused about the meaning. In item 2 the student clearly had a vocabulary problem, which also may be the case in item 3. The student seems to have gotten the key idea that rice is a safe crop, but seems to have thought that floods rather than droughts threaten the crop. The student was most likely confused about the meaning of drought, or it may be that the length of the sentence made it difficult for him to figure out the relations among the parts of the sentence. In item 4 the sentence leaves out what the natural conditions are responsible for. The good reader knows that something must be supplied and looks back to the previous sentence to achieve coherent understanding, however, this reader did not make that connection. And finally in item 5, the student interpreted Dutch rule literally as a set of rules. This may indicate a lack of knowledge about rule in the sense of governing and also about the particular relevance of Dutch governance in Indonesia.

Think-alouds work best with text that is a little unfamiliar to students. Usually it is easier to use informational texts rather than stories because often children's comprehension of stories is so automatic that they have difficulty verbalizing their thinking. Informational texts are usually less familiar than narratives in both content and structure. The unfamiliarity means that the reader's processing is less automatic and so it is easier to become aware of comprehension processes and talk about them. The usefulness of the technique depends on getting a text that is at an instructional level. If the text is too easy for a child, the think-aloud will be an adequate retelling and because he faces no problems you will gain little information about comprehension processes. If the text is too difficult, the child will be faced with so many problems that normal comprehension processing breaks down and the child will not be able to understand.

Steps for Gathering Think-Alouds

1. Select a 200- to 300-word instructional-level text that poses some comprehension challenges.

2. Explain to the child that when readers read, they are constantly thinking about what they are reading. Tell him you want him to tell you what he is thinking about as he is reading. For example:

> I am going to ask you to think aloud about this story as you are reading. When you come to a red mark, I want you to stop and tell me what you are thinking. For example, if I read the sentence, "About two-thirds of the people of Indonesia live on the island of Java," I would think, "Well, this is going to be about Indonesia and its people. And it tells me that most of the people live on Java." Then I would read the next bit, "the political heart of the country." I would think it makes sense that the place where most of the people are, Java, is the political center of the country. Now I want you to try the next sentence.

3. Practice taking turns with the child until you are sure he understands what to do.

4. Once you are sure that the child understands, let him complete the passage.

Tutors have several common problems with administering think-alouds. The first is that because the task is unfamiliar to both tutors and children, often both are not quite sure what they are to do. Tutors select an inappropriate text and then segment into sections that are too large. Because you want to observe the process of constructing meaning it is important to use small segments such as sentences, or when sentences are too long, clauses. The second problem is that when the child is confused, tutors automatically resort to asking the child questions and the think-aloud turns into a question-and-answer session. Instead of asking questions, the tutor should say, "Well, if I read that I would think..." and model the process again. If the tutor persists and models on his or her turn, offers the child a turn, and models again if the child does not succeed, continuing this cycle patiently, eventually the child will understand. Usually it does not take more than a paragraph or two for the child to catch on. The third problem is that the tutor often models a single comprehension strategy, such as restating the facts or predicting what will come next, and the child then uses a single strategy in his or her think-aloud. When you model think-alouds keep in mind the list of comprehension strategies in Figure 21 and use multiple strategies as they are appropriate.

Figure 21
Commonly Used Comprehension Strategies

- Always ask "does this make sense?"

- Predict what will come next.

- Check predictions to see if you are right.

- Reread to see if that helps you understand.

- Read ahead to see if the author gives information that will help you.

- Ask why the author is giving you this information.

- Draw comparisons between the text and your own life.

- Connect new information in the text to what you already know.

- See if an unfamiliar word may be related to a word that you know.

- Stop and see if you can state the author's major point.

- Explain why the author is using this order to present information.

- Substitute a known word that makes sense for an unknown word.

- Make sure you understand how drawings and tables go with the text.

- Ask how this information relates to earlier information.

SUMMARIZING

Good readers can summarize the essence of what they read. For example, a 99th percentile reader summarized the text like this:

> Java is an island in Indonesia, and it is real populous. It has over 60 million people and New York has 20 million and you think of that as being real populous only Java is smaller so they're crowded and they cannot spread out all over it because it is not habitable. But they've made a lot of it you know workable and livable because the rains wash down soil and they can grow rice and the Dutch sort of helped colonize Java, they had to get it started.

What characterizes this summary is that the reader drew the necessary inferences to identify the major points of the text selection. Note that although the original text only implies that Java is populous, this point is stated directly in the first sentence of the summary. He also realized that paragraphs two and three are providing reasons why Java is populous. So the reader followed the overall organization of the excerpt to guide the summarization. This reader's summary is exceptional, but the following is more typical of summaries produced by good readers:

> It is about the same size as New York. It has 60 million people. The Dutch helped influence population growth. They grow rice.

Although this summary is less complete, it does focus on the main ideas of the passage indicating that the student used the passage organization to sort important information from unimportant information. The summary does contain points related to the large populations, the Dutch role in population growth, and the rice that feeds the population.

The struggling readers' oral reports are organized poorly and presented illogically:

> There are 17 volcanoes that erupt. And Java is in Indonesia. And um and um Tells about when it rains that the soil washes off the volcanoes and down in to the lowlands for farming.

And here is another:

> Rice is a very good thing that they raise. And is it New York is smaller than what most people think it is? The people that live there and what they live on and how they live.

The reason that struggling readers select particular facts to report in their summaries is not immediately obvious, and the selection of information included does not appear to be influenced by the overall structure of the text.

Examining student summaries for their comprehension of major points and their sensitivity to the overall structure of the passage can provide important information about students' comprehension processes.

Steps for Gathering Summaries

1. Select an instructional-level text of about 200 to 300 words.
2. Briefly explain what a summary is: A short version of the text that tells its most important points.
3. Provide an example summary like the ones listed earlier.
4. Tell the student that she can develop a good summary by answering the question, "What is this text about?" with a simple phrase such as "Indonesia being very populous," and then explaining what the passage tells her about the phrase.
5. Allow the child to practice on some short passages that you read.
6. Collect the summary on an instructional-level passage.

RETELLING

Another technique that is used to evaluate comprehension is having students retell what they have read. Care must be taken in using this approach because students and tutors often misrepresent retelling as an exact reproduction of text. In actual reading tasks, exact reproduction of text is rarely the point. In my work with struggling readers I often have administered Informal Reading Inventories that use retelling as a comprehension measure (see Chapter 5 for further discussion of these inventories). Many of the children I tested were tested frequently, and I noticed that quite often when I gave the instruction to tell me about the story, they repeated the story nearly verbatim. In fact their retellings were much more complete than mine would have been. When I was working with one child I noticed that her reading rate was very slow and she was pausing for a long time at the end of each sentence. When I asked her what she was doing, she told me she was "trying to remember it." When I explained that I did not want her to memorize the story, but rather to just think about and understand it, her rate increased and her comprehension improved.

I am also cautious of retellings because of the message they send to teachers, tutors, and children about what is important in reading. One of my colleagues came to me after the school's annual reading tests wondering if he should ask his child to tell stories in complete detail after a story was read to him. He was asking because his child's teacher had noted that the child left many details out of his story retellings and suggested that my colleague work with the child so that he remembered more of the details. I doubt the value of such exercises and think that they may cause comprehension problems rather than result in any improvement.

With these cautions noted, retelling can help tutors evaluate a child's comprehension. Retelling is a task that adult readers do sometimes use, for example, when we tell someone a story that we have read or retell a story that someone has told us. Retellings are different from summaries because they include more detail and the intention is to recreate the story experience for someone else. Retelling stories also is useful because it can help us understand and remember stories better.

Steps for Collecting Retellings

1. Select a 200- to 300-word instructional-level text.
2. Explain briefly what a retelling is: A retelling is our own version of a story that we have heard or read. When we retell a story we want the listener to understand the story as we understood it when we read it.
3. Provide an example of retelling.
4. Allow the child to practice on some short passages that you read.
5. Collect the retelling on an instructional-level passage.

The information you gather from retellings and the other assessments can help you plan instruction. If you find that the child is merely calling words and thinks of reading as pronouncing words, you can begin to teach comprehension skills. Think-alouds can be used as an instructional technique as well as for assessment. The brief instruction done to introduce the Think-aloud task can be extended during mini-lessons. Also these assessments sometimes uncover specific areas of weakness such as lack of vocabulary knowledge or not understanding certain passage structures. All of these can be the topics of minilessons particularly for transition readers.

FOR THE SUPERVISOR

The concept of think-alouds is unfamiliar to many students and tutors. Their lack of familiarity sometimes makes using think-alouds difficult. However, I have found that having the tutor demonstrate thinking aloud first and then having the child and tutor alternate thinking aloud solves the problem. However, the tutor needs to provide a good model. If the tutor simply repeats sentences, the student will do the same without constructing meaning across sentences. In introducing think-alouds, it is good to review commonly used comprehension strategies such as those listed in Figure 21 and to model their use for the tutors in a demonstration think-aloud.

Tutors also may have trouble getting children to summarize, particularly if they have been trained to do retellings. Again modeling is useful. If when the tutor asks the question, What was this (story or text) about? and the child tells every detail, tell the tutor to explain that it is not necessary for the child to tell every single thing that he or she read, just tell the important things. And then have the tutor do a good summary of the text that the child has just retold. Sometimes tutors need help with summarizing themselves. You may need to spend training time explaining how passage structures can be used to select important information for inclusion in a summary. Most good methods texts, particularly those that deal with reading in the content areas, will have good information about teaching summarizing.

Sometimes children get caught up in reproducing stories verbatim when they are asked to do retellings. If this happens the tutor can model a retelling and then explain that the child does not have to use the exact words of the story, he or she just needs to convey what happens in the story to the listener. You may need to watch tutors carefully when they begin to use retellings. They too often think the point is exact recall and they are impressed when children can repeat every detail verbatim. You may have to remind them many times that verbatim repetition is not the point of retelling.

Chapter 8

Reading Easy Books

BUILDING UNDERSTANDING AND CONFIDENCE

Reading easy books is just that. During the reading easy books segment of the lesson children spend time reading books that that they can read successfully. The child should not be struggling to identify words during this part of the lesson. Traditional guidelines suggest that books should be read with 98% meaningful accuracy to be classified as easy. The child also should read the books at a comfortable rate with appropriate phrasing and intonation. For many readers, this level of comfort is not achievable on first reading and only books they have reread several times actually qualify as easy reading.

The purpose of easy reading is to give children who are struggling to read the experience of reading fluently and well. Many children who are tutored in reading have a sense of failure. They trudge through texts laboriously and slowly, wondering how other children read a page so quickly. They wonder why every word is a trial for them while other children seem able to comprehend whole sentences one after the other with hardly any work at all. Reading easy books has many benefits, but one of the most important is the sense of accomplishment and competence that results from reading fluently.

Rising Above the Words

The point of reading is to achieve meaning. Struggling readers have a hard time getting to this point because they must work so hard to understand the words.

Words are the major focus of almost everything struggling early readers read. Because they have very limited sight vocabulary, every word must be figured out. Often the only way to achieve a sense of ease with the words is to have the children reread familiar books. With each rereading they struggle with fewer words and more of their attention can be devoted to enjoying the books, commenting on meaning, and "sounding good." In 1992, I published a study of easy reading (Roller, 1992). I found that as children reread easy books, their accuracy increased and the amount of discussion between tutor and child decreased. For most of the children the amount of talk devoted to figuring out words decreased. When the children stopped concentrating primarily on saying the words, their focus shifted to discussing the meaning, developing speed, or sounding good, or sometimes shifted to another facet of reading they were working on.

All of these goals are important for early readers. The importance of focusing on meaning hardly needs to be mentioned. Children who read without grasping meaning are not really reading at all. Although speed and sounding good may seem less critical, they are important for several reasons. First, early struggling readers want desperately to read well. Often their conception of reading well, like that of many second- and third-grade children, is to read *fast*. Second, reading fast and sounding good are informal names for fluency, and fluency is important because it is associated closely with comprehension. In general, fluent readers comprehend well and slow laborious readers comprehend less well.

All too often, however, fluency is equated with speed and accuracy rather than with comprehension. I notice this particularly with second- and third-grade children. Often the best readers in the class will speed through a text so quickly that no one listening has any notion of what was read. Research, which often measures fluency in terms of rate and accuracy, has helped to perpetuate this misconception. Fluency should be defined not only as reading fast and accurately, but also as reading with appropriate phrasing and intonation. Fluent readers "sound good" because they group words together into sensible phrases and because they use their voices to emphasize some words while de-emphasizing others. Their voices indicate the ends of sentences or questions with rising and falling intonation patterns.

To understand how fluency is related to comprehension, read the poem on the following page aloud several times.

Two Voices in a Meadow
Richard Wilbur (1961)

A Milkweed

Anonymous as cherubs
Over the crib of God,
White seeds are floating
Out of my burst pod.
What power had I
Before I learned to yield?
Shatter me, great wind:
I shall possess the field.

The Stone

As casual as cow-dung
Under the crib of God,
I lie where chance would have me,
Up to my ears in sod.
Why should I move? To move
Befits a light desire.
The sill of heaven would founder,
Did such as I aspire.

Most readers find that with each rereading they understand the poem better, and they also change their phrasing and intonation to reflect their growing understanding.

MOTIVATING EASY READING

Some children enjoy rereading easy books; others do not. I am always thankful for those who do because with them, the first part of the lesson goes smoothly and well. However, when children do not enjoy rereading easy books there are several strategies tutors can use to motivate them (Fielding & Roller, 1992; Forbes & Roller, 1991; Roller & Fielding, 1996). Usually when children resist reading easy books it is because they perceive a stigma attached to reading the books, the books are not interesting, or both. In addition, children sometimes resist rereading because they cannot see the point and will simply say, "We already did that!"

I have found that particularly in tutoring, when the child is not in the presence of peers, there is less resistance to reading easy books. However, I have found that some children in our SRP tutoring program resist strongly. In previous writing I have quoted Heidi and Mark (Fielding & Roller, 1992; Forbes & Roller, 1991; Roller, 1996; Roller & Fielding, 1996):

> Heidi: I don't like to read easy books. They're BAAAAABY books and they're BOOOR-RRING.

> Mark: Easy books. EEEasy books. They're all so boring. All so boring. I don't like to read easy books. I think the reason why you read is to...hear interesting stories. I don't like reading easy books. Don't usually have much in them.

Modeling adult enjoyment of easy books, reading to younger children, preparing audiotapes for other children, preparing for Readers Theatre (described on page 116), recording speed and accuracy on rereadings, and having children read books they have authored themselves can all contribute to motivating easy reading.

Modeling Adult Enjoyment

Not all easy books are boring. In fact some of the easiest books are sometimes quite amusing. I remember the first time I read *Don't You Laugh At Me* (Cowley, 1980a). I literally laughed out loud when I read, "But spider couldn't stop laughing. So bird ate him." It surprised me, I was not expecting the simple force of "So bird ate him." Circular patterns, such as those in *The Bee* (Cowley, 1981) and *Come and Talk to Me* (Cowley, 1992), are intrinsically appealing and entertaining. For example, on his first reading of *Come and Talk to Me*, Andrew was delighted at the end when he realized that no one could talk to the little girl because each one thought another animal was chasing him or her.

> Andrew: (reading the page that completes the circle) No, no. A bug is after me.
>
> Tutor: Good!
>
> Andrew: It just went in a circle!
>
> Tutor: Yeah.
>
> Andrew: Bug thought the bird that was coming back and the cat thought, the bird thought the cat was chasing it, the dog thought the cow she,

See it? (pointing to the picture) And the cow thought he was gonna get chased caught by the boy and the boy he was gonna get caught by the bug. But all because of the little bug, the mom made all that!

Tutor: You're right!

Andrew: They just kept on going in a circle! They went in a circle.

Tutor: What happened to the boy? They sure did. It just ended up in a big circle!

Some easy books with repetitive patterns have human themes underlying them and although the books are easy, the themes are not. For example, consider *The Three Billy Goats Gruff* (Asbjornsen, 1973) which pits cleverness against brute force, or *Mrs. Wishy Washy* (Cowley, 1987) which plays on the futility of trying to make animals behave in ways that are contrary to their nature. In previous writing I have quoted excerpts from an animated discussion that my SRP 8- to 12-year-olds had about *Mrs. Wishy Washy* (Forbes & Roller, 1991) and about Colin West's *Have You Seen the Crocodile?* (1986) (*Variability Not Disability*, pp. 59–61).

Reading With Younger Children

Another strategy we use at SRP is having the children read to younger children. This can be very effective and it can be a disaster. In 1996 the SRP children were studied as they read to young children at a nearby day-care center (Young, 1996). Most of the children had good experiences. Their teacher took time to prepare them for the visit. The children talked about choosing good books—ones that would hold the younger children's attention, that would fill the right amount of time, and that they could read well. They practiced and prepared the books they would read. Their teacher had them set goals for their reading and write them down prior to each day-care visit. They also wrote responses to the visits in their journals and most of these were positive. Megan's and Charlie's responses show the importance of the younger child's reaction to these visits:

Megan: I liked the little kids. I liked how they all came up to you. I had two little kids. They were so sweet. I had a girl and a boy. The little girl did not talk. The boy talked the whole time. He liked horses. He would not let me read about anything else. He was cute though.

Charlie: I really like going to the Day Care because three other kids came up to me and started listening to me before I go back. I'm going to get a better book and say it better. (p. 11)

On one or two occasions the SRP children were embarrassed when very young children corrected their reading. For example, Randy, a beginning reader, was paired with a child who could read the books Randy had chosen. Randy was not as well prepared as he should have been because the day before the day-care visit he decided he was tired of his books and traded them for news ones that he had not read. At several points the young boy read along with Randy in a whisper and if Randy stumbled or read a word incorrectly the child sometimes corrected him. Randy was devastated. When asked what he thought about the day-care visits he said he would rather just read at SRP by himself, " 'cause then you can decide if you need help or not." Randy's experience demonstrates that no technique is foolproof. The success of reading with younger children depends on careful planning and preparation on the part of children and teachers.

After studying the day-care experience, Young (1996) made several recommendations that included:

- model and discuss ways to share books with young children
- have the children set goals and reflect on performance
- have the children practice books until they are mastered
- match children carefully
- space visits to allow enough preparation time

Recording Books for Others

Preparing audiotapes for other children or adults to listen to is a very popular activity at SRP. Because the children have the opportunity to read and listen and retape themselves, they often practice books many more times than they would otherwise and because sounding good on the tape is important to them, they often choose easy books. Their concern with sounding good seems to eclipse their resistance to easy books.

Book selection is critical for this activity. The children must be reading books that are easy enough so that with two or three readings they can achieve fluency. It also helps for the children to have a particular audience in mind. Sometimes children enjoy preparing tapes for their parents or for younger siblings. School classes are also good audiences, and taping books for children in lower grades works well. Sending tapes to a younger child who is not nearby is also a possibility. It also helps to give the child control over the tape recorder and allow them to erase and retape as often as they wish. The more times they erase, the more practice they get reading.

Readers Theatre

Readers Theatre, which is reading a script for a live audience, is another effective way to motivate easy reading and rereading. The children know that performance requires practice and consequently they are willing to reread a passage many times. Stayter and Allington (1991) report a sequence of reading behaviors that occurred as children were preparing for Readers Theatre. They noted that the children's first readings varied widely and that some of the struggling readers had a tendency to read in funny voices or to use unusual rhythm patterns, probably to mask their discomfort with oral reading. As days went by, their reading became more fluent; it reflected their growing understanding of the parts they were reading. The children commented on how their reading changed with growing understanding. They talked about changing their opinions of characters and understanding why characters behaved as they did.

Simple plays also can motivate easy reading. Each summer I leave sets of four or five early basal readers (texts designed for developmental reading) on the bottom shelf of the book case. Sometimes the children will select these to read to a small group because the pieces found at the earlier levels are written as plays with cartoon drawings of characters to identify who is speaking. The children like being able to read these plays. Providing opportunities for performance in tutoring programs can help motivate easy reading.

Charting Rate and Accuracy

Another strategy to encourage fluent reading, timing children for rate and accuracy, should be used with caution. Rereading a text almost always improves children's speed and accuracy; it helps them read faster and focus on meaning. Rate improves and errors are reduced and become more meaning based. Children like to time themselves and to keep track of their improvement and you can help them do this if it seems useful. However, this strategy can be used in some detrimental ways. For example, sometimes only rate and accuracy are charted and other strategies for fluent reading are ignored. Over time the goal becomes increasing speed and decreasing mistakes. The real goal of fluency, to read in a way that reflects the meaning of the text, gets lost.

117

Reading Your Own Writing

Having struggling readers read their own writing is a time-honored remedial technique (Fernald, 1943). It makes sense that reading text you have written yourself is easier than reading text written by others. You cannot write words you do not know the meaning of and about topics you know nothing about. You are likely to use sentence patterns and text structures that are familiar. Furthermore, you are likely to write and about topics that interest you. All of these factors make it easier for you to identify words and hence self-authored texts are often a good choice for easy reading.

EMERGENT READERS

Easy reading with emergent readers can be tricky. Because they have limited sight vocabularies and often are reading in patterned text, their reading is sometimes recitation. I have written elsewhere (Forsyth & Roller, in press; also see Chapter 9, p. 128) of Brandi who after reading a book three times announced proudly, "I can read it without looking." The pleasure the child takes in reading fluently and well is important and we should not underestimate the importance of being able to "sound good" to many struggling readers. Tutors should not overreact to memorized text or belabor this part of the lesson by focusing their attention solely on words. However, it probably is also important to limit this kind of easy reading to very short (probably not more than 5 minutes) segments of the tutoring session. Other parts of the lesson can focus on attending to print and to building understanding of print's function in reading.

Peter was an 11-year-old child still reading below a preprimer level. He had a history of language delay and impairment. Peter's easy-reading sessions are a typical example of easy-reading sessions for older emergent readers. Over a 5-week period he reread 4 books a total of 14 times—*Brown Bear, Brown Bear, What Do You See?* (Martin, 1983) 5 times, *Little Red Hen* (Cowley, 1980b) 3 times, *Numbers* (Youlden, 1984) 3 times, and 2 pages of *One Fish Two Fish Red Fish Blue Fish* (Seuss, 1960) 3 times. In general, with each reading he became more accurate and talked less with his tutor. Most of the talk that did occur was either about words (that is, how to remember that the book said *cottages* rather than *houses*) or about procedures (that is, discussions about what and how they would read).

The most striking feature of Peter's rereadings was the lack of talk about meaning. One might surmise that he did not talk about the books because he did not like them or because he did not understand them. However, records from lesson plans and supervisor's notes indicate that neither was the case. Peter was generally enthusiastic about the books. His tutor reported that he was extremely disappointed when she did not bring *Little Red Hen* and begged her to bring it for a third reading. When she introduced *Brown Bear, Brown Bear*, he immediately wanted to read it. And he often shared similar books in SRP's morning classroom.

It is clear from the tutor's lesson evaluations that Peter did understand the books. One evaluation reported, "Peter obviously understands what is happening is this book. He made comments about how the hen deserved all of the cake because she did all of the work." Other clinic documents also indicate that Peter understood the books he read.

I think that Peter and his tutor both understood the rereading segment of the lesson as a place to focus on fluency. Peter was enthusiastic about these books because he could read them, and he was willing to reread them because he liked "sounding good." I also think Peter and his tutor viewed reading easy books as a chance to read fast and accurately. This is substantiated by Peter's request, granted by his tutor, to time his reading of *Brown Bear*. Fluency is an important achievement for struggling emergent readers.

BEGINNING READERS

Beginning readers can read text that is a bit more complex and it is here that we begin to observe what happens as children gain control of decoding—they focus on meaning. Jason and his tutor read two texts three times each: *Jesse Bear, What Will You Wear?* (Carlstrom, 1986) and *Curious George Plays Baseball* (Rey & Rey, 1986). His accuracy in both books increased from 91% on the first reading to 98% in the third reading. Talk about pronouncing words decreased across readings as talk about meaning increased. An example from the initial to final readings of *Jesse Bear* shows how Jason's and his tutor's attention shifted from decoding to meaning.

The text of *Jesse Bear* consists of 18 segments that answer the question of the title, "Jesse Bear, what will you wear?" On the first reading Jason and his tutor talked during 17 of the 18 segments and pronouncing words was a part of each discussion. For eight of the segments there was discussion in both the first and final readings. Initially however, all eight of the discussions included talk about pronouncing words and only three included talk about the meaning of the text. On the final reading, seven of the discussions included talk about meaning. Here is an example of the discussions on the first and the final readings of one of the text segments. The text read: *I'll wear my pants, my pants that dance in the morning.* On the first reading Jason read, "I'm walking" for *I'll wear.*

His tutor asked, "Do you want to try that again?"

He did try it, "I'll wear my pants, my pants," and he hesitated on *that,* finally calling it "what."

His tutor corrected him and he continued, "that pa (pause) dance."

His tutor encouraged, "Um hm," and Jason finished, "my pants that dance in the morning."

In this initial reading, the tutor's comments were either responses to errors or confirmations of correct words. On the final reading Jason read the segment without error, and his tutor asked, "How do pants dance?"

Jason answered, "Well, he's dancing and his pants move because they're on his legs."

"Um hm," answered his tutor. "Do you have any clothes that you wear that make you feel just kind of perky and happy?"

"Yeah."

"I do too! That's neat isn't it."

In the final reading Jason and his tutor talked less and when they talked, they primarily discussed the book's meaning rather than word pronunciation. This shift to focusing on meaning is a critical accomplishment for beginning readers.

TRANSITION READERS

Transition readers have finally reached the point where they can read fairly complex text. Susan, another SRP student, was reading *The Long Blue Blazer* (Willis, 1987). She read the book five times. Her accuracy increased from 96% on the first three readings to 98% on the last two, and her focus on decoding went down across readings with the exception of the second reading during which 78% of the talk was focused on meaning and only 1% on decoding. What Susan's data showed was that her tutor had very specific and different purposes on each rereading. On the second reading during which 78% of the talk was focused on meaning, her tutor was a bit concerned about Susan not wanting to reread the book. In this session she chose not to focus on decoding words and instead had lively discussions of what was happening in the book. The following excerpt is typical of their talk during this reading.

Susan: The last I ever saw of him is [was] his long blue tail. His long blue tail?

Tutor: She just realized he had a

Susan: Tail.

Tutor: And we could write on this page, *And so did his*

Susan: *And so did* his mother.

Tutor: Yeah!

The discussion went on for many more turns as they discussed the story and illustrations. Susan evidently enjoyed the session and the book because she chose to read it three more times. On the third and fourth reading the data suggest that the focus of the talk shifted back to words. However, a closer examination of the transcripts suggests another agenda.

On the third reading of *Long Blue Blazer*, the tutor paid very little attention to meaning. There were 24 short discussions during this reading—14 initiated by the tutor, 10 by Susan. The discussions Susan initiated were mainly short interruptions; however, four discussions were focused on meaning. Her tutor, on the other hand, initiated no discussions related to meaning. She focused on specific words, asking questions like, "What was this word?" or "What was this?" and often she read one or two words to restart Susan. A focus on language came up several times. For example, the tutor commented on the /e/ sound of *y*. She mentioned, "Oh good! More than one!" when Susan said a plural *-s*. At another point she commented "good one of those *-ing* words. " The transcript suggests that attending to inflectional endings was a major focus in the third reading. This focus continued in the fourth reading. This probably was useful because Susan had a history of language delay and still was not using correct inflectional endings consistently. The tutor's comments were very brief and did not disrupt the flow of the story.

In the final reading there was almost no discussion. Susan read fluently and accurately and both her comments and her tutor's were focused on how well she was doing:

Susan: Oh this is so easy. I don't know. I only know my times.

Tutor: You know your times too? Besides your addition and subtraction!

Susan: Yay! That's the end.

Tutor: That's the end. You're just reading that one better every time aren't you! You get almost every word right now every time!

Susan and the tutor discussed the book thoroughly during the second reading. During the remaining readings there was very little extraneous talk. The tutor used the third and fourth readings to reinforce the pronunciation of inflectional endings in very quick comments praising Susan. In the final reading the talk centered around how fluent the readings were. Easy reading for transition readers often focuses on meaning, but occasionally focuses briefly on some other goal. Sometimes there is very little talk all.

FOR THE SUPERVISOR

The easy reading segment of session usually goes fairly well and both tutor and child enjoy it because it highlights the child's competence. However, sometimes children resist rereading and it is important to solve this problem early by using some of the techniques I mentioned in the "Motivating Easy Reading" section of this chapter. Tutors should be encouraged to persist even if their student does not like this section of the lesson.

The other problem I often encounter in easy reading is that the tutor just cannot stop using each mistake as an opportunity for teaching. I think this is because they do not separate the purposes of the easy reading and reading the new book segments of the lesson. In addition, the idea that a part of the lesson should be devoted to enjoyment and fun sometimes runs counter to a tutor's intuitive sense that during one-on-one tutoring the child should be taking advantage of all learning opportunities. During early tutoring sessions I emphasize that there is no point in teaching a child to read if we do not teach them to *want* to read.

Chapter 9

Reading the New Book

THE HEART OF THE TUTORING SESSION

Reading the new book is the most important activity in the tutoring session. Handerhan (1990) studied excellent Reading Recovery tutors. She found that the most effective tutor spent more than twice the time on the new book activity than did a less effective tutor. Reading the new book means that the child reads a book to the tutor and the tutor helps in appropriate ways. Hopefully, after reading Chapter 4 and reading this chapter, you will understand the ways of helping that are appropriate. Probably about one third of a tutoring session should be spent reading a new book. Carefully selected new books provide just the right kind and number of opportunities for learning and practicing new skills.

Appropriate Difficulty Level

Reading the new book provides opportunities to learn, use, and practice the many complex skills of reading. The tutor operates like a coach who provides important cues and help at critical points. The difficulty level of a book is much like the skill level of an opposing team. If the opposition is weak your team will breeze through the game and learn little. If the opposition is a good match, your team will work hard and be stretched to use skills that are just maturing. If the opposition is much better, your team may be so overwhelmed that they become dispirited and discouraged and actually lose confidence in their skills.

In the new book activity, the book and the child should be a good match. Traditional wisdom suggests that students should be able to read 90% to 95% of the words without help and should understand what they have read. Tutors decide whether the child understands by asking questions or asking the child to retell the story. They usually make an intuitive judgment about whether the child has understood, but sometimes they actually prepare a list of questions and decide that the child has understood if he or she can answer 60% to 70% of them.

The 90% to 95% level of accuracy is often a surprise to those outside the reading field. In schools most passing scores are set at 70% or 80%. Our intuitive sense is that 80% is pretty good. One way to understand why 90% to 95% is important in reading is to block out nouns, verbs, adjectives, and adverbs in a text and then try to read. You will find that with 90% to 95% of the words intact it is still possible to figure out the message; however, once you have fewer than 90% of the words available the task becomes much harder. In fact some authorities insist on a 95% to 98% level rather than the 90% to 95% because research findings suggest that good readers usually read with at least that level of accuracy. As a guideline, if a child is missing 1 or 2 words in 20 and is understanding the book, the difficulty level is probably the right level for learning. You probably need to keep running records on children's reading to make sure that they are reading at this level of accuracy because tutors usually tolerate much lower levels for struggling readers. This tolerance may contribute to their struggle.

In Chapter 4 I noted that it is important to keep a lesson moving. This is another reason that books that allow for high levels of accuracy are necessary. Too many unfamiliar words slow down the lesson. Sometimes children lose the meaning of what they are reading and stumble so many times that they cannot remember the beginning of a sentence by the time they get to the end of it.

I am often amazed at teachers' and tutors' commitment to finishing what they start. They seem determined to finish each task and they often do not notice how frustrated a child is becoming. If they do notice, they try to provide praise and encouragement as the child sighs, twists his hair, or gently pounds on the table. I have seen tutors persist until a child is in tears. Tutors need to tune into the child's emotional signals because these frequently tell when the lesson is lagging. When an activity is frustrating the child, you need to make changes. Usually this means putting aside the particular book or reading part or all of it to the child so that you can move on to a more productive activity. If you are careful to work in books at the right difficulty level, however, you can avoid this problem.

Choice

Although choice creates motivation for children to read, in this part of the tutoring session we cannot give the children unlimited choice because the difficulty level of the book is so critical to the success of the activity. However, we still can provide *some* choice. We can bring to the sessions a selection of books that are *all* at an appropriate difficulty level. And we can use all of the resources available, including material the tutor or child has written to make sure that there are several books available that are interesting to the child. I do not mean to suggest this is easy—particularly if the child is older and is still reading at very early stages. But there are many easy books being published today. The "Resources" section at the end of *Variability Not Disability* will give you some ideas about how to find them. Interest is important. Children will work much harder to read books that they actually want to read.

Wait Time

Wait time gives the child a chance to perform, and is thus a very important concept. Often waiting longer for the child's responses is the single most important change required of tutors. When you are working with a child who is struggling, you want to help and many times the child who is struggling wants help. So the instant the child encounters trouble you jump in. But think about the message jumping in sends to the child. It says, "Oh no! You cannot do this!" This is the one message we do not want to send. To avoid it, tutors can make sure that the child is using "just right" books. When the child has difficulty, tutors should wait a minimum of 3 to 5 seconds to give her a chance to solve the problem.

This wait time issue can be difficult—particularly with children who are used to getting help immediately. If a child has learned that adults always help with hard words, you may, for a while, have to wait even longer to convey to the child that you expect that he or she will be able to do it independently. I worked with one child who would come up with the answer if I waited 8 to 13 seconds. However, we cannot wait forever and we cannot let the lesson bog down too much. If you are working with a child who simply wants to wait you out, you will probably have to emphasize with additional direct instruction what you expect her to do when she comes to a word she does not know.

When to Ignore, When to Help, When to Tell

Knowing when to ignore children's errors, when to help, and when to tell words is the essence of reading tutoring. In the examples that follow I will point out the particular decision points and discuss reasons for making a particular decision. In this section I will provide some generally accepted guidelines.

Ignore errors that do not change the meaning of the story. The most important reason for tutors to ignore these mistakes is that the child should depend on meaning to monitor his or her reading. Skilled readers only stop and correct themselves when reading is not making sense to them. If we stop children at every single error, such as when they say *the* for *a*, or say *mushrooms* when the text says *some* meaning the mushrooms, we send the message that accuracy is what is important. Accuracy is not the most important aspect of reading. Understanding is the essence; we only identify words so we can understand. Ignoring errors that do not change meaning also helps keep the lesson moving.

Teach at only a few key places where the child can learn what he or she most needs to learn. Tutors should not take every hesitation and miscue as an opportunity to teach the child. First, limit the number of hesitations and miscues by reading in "just right" books. Second, know what the child knows about reading, what the child is learning, and what the child needs to learn next. Tutors should understand reading development (see Chapter 3) and should have carefully observed the child's reading, perhaps looking at running records and talking with teachers and parents to really understand this particular child. Intimate knowledge of the child and the reading process enables tutors to make good decisions about what to teach and when to teach it. In the examples at the end of this chapter I will describe children at the emergent, beginning, and transition stages to help you get a sense of how to decide when and what to teach.

Sometimes it is OK to tell the word and sometimes it is not OK. One striking finding of research on tutor-child interaction during oral reading is that tutors working with struggling readers interrupt immediately and tell the child the word. The most likely reasons for this are that tutors do not want the child to struggle and be embarrassed and they want to keep the lesson moving. When tutors work with better readers they do not interrupt as frequently and they do not tell the word as often— probably because they have confidence that these children can tell when they need to correct and will be able to do it on their own.

However, one mistake tutors of struggling readers make after reading or hearing about this research is *never* telling the children the word. They will wait and ask questions and give hints until the child gets the word. What happens is that the lesson bogs down and the child gets frustrated. What the tutor should do instead is give the child enough wait time to make an attempt, perhaps offering a few prompts, and if the child is not successful, tell the word. It is important to give the child the opportunity because many times she can be successful if she is not interrupted, but it is foolish to allow frustration to enter the lesson because of single words.

Tutors also should tell words that are not in a child's speaking vocabulary. Tutors get to know the child they work with very well because they concentrate on the child for large segments of time. Often they know what words are in the child's vocabulary and what words are not. For example, there would be no point in working on the word *flannel* if you knew the child had no experience with flannel and did not have the word in her speaking vocabulary. Even if she said the word correctly, she would not *know* the word. The better strategy is to say, "That word is flannel. In the north, where it gets very cold, they make sheets and pajamas out of a flannel material that is soft and cozy and warm. It is called flannel—a kind of soft cloth."

Multiple Flexible Strategies

By now you realize that reading involves using multiple strategies in complex and flexible ways. This complexity is one of the reasons that reading many books with a tutee is the best way to teach reading. Reading cannot be broken down into simple easy parts that can be put together in a certain order to produce a reader. Children sometimes need to focus on specific aspects of reading because they do not know them or are having trouble with them. However, if we only focus on these aspects and do not use them in actual reading, then children often do not understand how to use what they know when they read. Remember Randy who could not read the word *clever*. He kept saying, *clo, clo, clo*. Yet when I asked him if he knew vowel sounds, he reeled them off in a single breath. He knew the sounds, but he was not using the sounds during reading.

When we actually read books with children, we can decide what to teach because the text offers opportunities that match what the child knows or does not know. Sometimes it makes sense to sound out a word, sometimes the context is helpful, and sometimes the picture can help. Children need to learn when to use each of these strategies. Probably one of the most important lessons they need to

127

learn is, "If one thing is not working, try something else." Throughout all our teaching we should keep in mind that the objective is to teach the child multiple strategies and to be flexible in their use. The lists of minilessons in Chapter 11 can give you a sense of the kinds of strategies readers need to learn.

EMERGENT READERS

Conceptions of Reading

Emergent readers often have partial concepts of what reading is. They may think that reading is telling a story that goes with the pictures, that reading is remembering the words that go with the story, or that reading is sounding musical and fluent. They may not understand how print works, or know they should read from the top to the bottom of the page, and from left to right across the line. They may not even follow the lines. Often they do not understand what printed words are, and they do not know that words are made up of letters that represent sounds. The tutor's job with an emergent reader is to bring him or her closer to a full understanding of what reading is. The emergent reader needs to understand that the words he or she says must match the print on the page, and that the letters in the words have sounds that go together.

Brandi is a wonderful example of a child whose conception of reading was quite different from my own. The following dialogue represents an exchange I had with her. Earlier in the session I had read *The Boogley* (Cowley, 1980c) with her. She had read it fluently and well, and consistently said *comes* when the print said *came*. I had ignored the errors because they did not change the meaning and *comes* and *came* are fairly close to each other in letters and sounds. But when she finished the book I called her attention to the letters and sounds.

Cathy: OK, on this Boogley thing, you did a real nice job. I have a question for you though. Every time you saw this word (pointing to *came*) you said, *comes*. Can this be *comes*?

Brandi: Come (pause) *came*.

Brandi read a few pages correctly and then began another book. As she began I said, "Now I want you to look at the words on the page." Later in the session we had this exchange:

Brandi: Um, I read this book three times.

Cathy: Good for you. Are you good at it now?

Brandi: Yeah

Cathy: Great!

Brandi: I can read it without looking!

Cathy: Well, that's not good. I don't want you to read without looking because reading means *looking*.

(Brandi started to read her book to me but I interrupted.)

Cathy: See Brandi. I don't want you to memorize the book, I want you to read the book. So don't try to memorize the book. Try to watch the letters.

Brandi: OK

You can see from this exchange that I think the most important thing for Brandi to learn is to make a word-print match and to match the sounds and letters she says to the words on the page.

One of the things I do with children who do not seem to understand that what they say has to match the print is have them point to the words. When they point, they begin to notice the mismatch. For example, Matt was reading *The Bee* (Cowley, 1990). It is a patterned book that follows the progress of a bee. Each page has a picture that shows where the bee is, and the print reads, *In a* _____. Although he made several errors on the content words, I ignored them. In each case the word he said was similar in meaning and beginning letters. He was reading the *in a* pages well, but halfway through the book the pattern changed to *out of the*. Matt read, "out the" and went back when he realized there were too many words in the text. He reread, "out of the flower," and I commented, "Oh now, that was something that the finger helps with. Because what...what you did there was a really good thing. You went *out the flower*. You ran out of words right? So what did you do?" Because word-print match is an important concept for emergent readers, it was important to call Matt's attention to how using his finger helped him to match the words on the page to the words he said.

He continued reading and when he came to the word *after* he first called it "and" but immediately corrected to "after." I asked, "How did you know it was *after* and not *and*?" When I got no response I said, "Say *and*." Matt did, and he indicated he could hear the *d* at the end of *and* and it was not at the end of *after* so he knew he needed to change. Matt may have made the correction because *after* made sense and *and* did not, but I was focusing on making the match among words and letters and sounds.

In each of these cases I was trying to get the children to notice the relation between print and words and call their attention to the use of the letter sounds at the beginnings and ends of words. Because these children were reading simple patterned books, I often did the teaching after they had completed a page or sometimes even the whole book. Hopefully these examples help you see how tutors decide when and what they will teach. For example, with a child beyond the emergent stage who I am confident is making a word-print match, I probably would not do much teaching on Brandi's *comes* and *came* confusion because the incorrect reading did not affect the meaning. Had I been confident that she understood the need for words and print to match, I would have simply let the errors go. However, I was fairly sure she did not understand this important concept, so at the end of the lesson I called her attention to the miscue. Likewise, I took advantage of Matt's self-corrections to call his attention to the good skills he was using.

Introducing the Book

Another important feature of reading the new book with emergent readers is introducing the book. A good introduction to the book will help many children read books that they could not read otherwise. For example, I wanted to read the book *I See You* (Williams, 1992a) with Ken, but I knew that it had many words that might give him problems. The book has a repetitive sentence pattern: *I see you [animal] hiding in the [place]*. During the book introduction I made sure I used the words *bullfrog, dragonfly, reeds, lily pad, rocks, flowers, bush,* and *trees,* and I made sure he understood the pattern of the text.

Cathy:	What do you notice about these two pages? (pause) The words.
Ken:	They're the same but these two aren't.
Cathy:	Right—there are words that are the same and there are words that are different. So what words are always the same here?
Ken:	(points to each of the words that are the same.)
Cathy:	You sure have got it. And then these two words (pointing to the words) always change don't they?

Ken:	Um hm.
Cathy:	OK. So it'll be really important to see if we can figure out these words. Do you know them? (pause) Which ones do you know? Point to the ones you know.
Ken:	I see you (pause)
Cathy:	Just skip that one.
Ken:	In the water, I see you turtle don't know in in in the rocks.
Cathy:	OK. Now let's think about, this is the one word that you are struggling with. OK. Now if you were alone and by yourself...
Ken:	Hiiiii ding, hiding.
Cathy:	You did a good job on that. So I think you're gonna be able to read that book as long as we make sure we know the pattern .

During the reading I told Ken the words *reed* and *minnow*, and I ignored several instances where he said *on* instead of *in*. At the end of the reading I reviewed several words because I knew that this was a book Ken would read at the day-care center. I pointed to *minnow*.

Ken:	Minnow.
Cathy:	Minnow and um you got, Where was the word that I was kind of wondering how you did it? How did you, how did you know *bush*?
Ken:	Cause you told me it was a bush.
Cathy:	Was there anything else? Do you check the print? (pause) Say *bush* for me.
Ken:	Bush.
Cathy:	What do you hear when you say *bush*?
Ken:	/b/
Cathy:	And what do you hear at the end?
Ken:	/ush/.
Cathy:	/ush/. And does this match it? Do those letters go with those sounds?
Ken:	Yes. bbbbuuuuuuu uuush.
Cathy:	That's a kind of checking I want you to do. 'Cause that will help you learn. And I noticed that sometimes [pointing to *in*]

Ken:	In on.
Cathy:	OK. Now I want you to read this for me again.
Ken:	I see you hid bullfrog hiding in a lily pad. It should be *on*.
Cathy:	It should be *on* but the text says *in*, doesn't it?
	(Ken spontaneously reread most of the story saying *in* correctly)
Cathy:	I like the way you paid attention. 'Cause this really. He really isn't *in* the rocks. He's *on* the rocks.
Ken:	He's on.
Cathy:	But you looked at the print, didn't you. And you got the word that was there. Good for you.

Notice that I focused on teaching related to paying attention to the print and did most of the teaching at the end of the activity. Notice also that I sometimes told words such as *minnow* and *reed* that I did not think would be familiar. I also did not correct *on* for *in* while he read because in many cases his wording made more sense than the actual text wording. I did, however, call attention to it afterward because I wanted him to pay attention to print. Book introductions like this one prepare struggling readers for reading so that when they actually attempt reading the whole book, they are more likely to be successful. Indeed, some struggling emergent readers could read nothing at all if they were not supported by a book introduction.

BEGINNING READERS

The task with beginning readers is to get them to put all of the strategies they know together. Usually they understand what reading is and they make a word-print match. They know how letters and sounds go together, and they know many strategies for figuring out words. But making everything work together is hard for them. (For a review of some of the information about letters and sounds and strategies that skilled readers use for word recognition and comprehension, see Chapter 2.) Randy, who knew his short vowel sounds but did not use them to sound out *clever*, is a good example. Tommie is another. I talk about Tommie as an example of a beginning reader in *Variability Not Disability* (pp. 118–120). He was reading the book *Sheep in a Jeep* (Shaw, 1986) and we began the activity by talking about the book. Tommie had read part of it with someone else, so for an introduction he summarized what he had already read and then began reading. The page was about the sheep getting stuck on a steep hill. He had some trouble with *steep* and called it *sheep*. First, I asked him how the word was different from *sheep* and Tommie answered that the *t* and the *h* were different. I asked him to put the *st* sound at the beginning but he was still stuck.

Cathy: And think about hill. What can a hill be?

Tommie: Steep.

Cathy: Yeah. See how thinking about what it means can really help you when sounding out isn't doing very well? OK. Keep going.

A little while later he was trying to read the sentence, "Sheep leap to push the jeep. Sheep grunt." He could not figure out *grunt*. First I asked him to think about what the sheep were doing and he said shoving and shoving. Then I asked him to try to think of something that made sense that started with *gr*, but neither strategy worked.

Cathy: Now another thing you can do is read on. So just skip it.

Tommie: Sheep don't think to look *for, brunt, grunt.*

Cathy: Front. OK. so...

Notice that I quickly gave him *front*. Because we already were struggling with *grunt* it did not make sense to struggle with *front* too.

Tommie: Sheep don't think to look up front.

Cathy: OK, now you know that this book rhymes a lot. Can you go back and get that other page?

Tommie: Sheep shove, sheep dog dash.

Cathy: OK. It needs to rhyme with *front*.

Tommie: Unt unt...

Cathy: You say the *unt* I'll say the *gr*. (There was a short interruption.)

Tommie: Grunt.

Cathy: Grunt. Do you know what *grunt* is? OK. It's like grunt and groan.

In one sense this is probably an exchange that went on for too long, but it does show the complexity of integrating all the strategies that Tommie has available to him. At the end of the lesson I gave the summary on the following page.

OK, this is a good choice. Um, when you are reading by yourself, OK? Try to do some of the things we did. Read ahead. Think about the meaning. The meaning really helped you when you were...And here you said *sheep*, when we were talking about the hill? But then you thought about what a hill could be and you got *steep*? And here I didn't even do anything. You, it didn't make sense to you. You said *lamp* and it was *leap* and you went right back and made it say the right thing. I think partly because you knew *lamp* didn't make sense and partly because you knew it had to rhyme with *jeep—leap-jeep*. And *grunt*...that one, if you don't know the meaning of a word you're not likely to be able to figure it out. Those are the kind of words you need to come and ask me...And I want you to be thinking, "OK. What am I learning?" And some of the things that you should be able to learn from this book are that thinking about the meaning really helps, rhyming can help sometimes, and that rereading helps. So those are some of the things that you are learning.

TRANSITION READERS

Transition readers are fairly independent and they find many books that they actually can read. They need to make several transitions: the transition from oral to silent reading, the transition from picture books to books with mostly text, and the transition from storybooks to expository or informational books. In the examples that follow I will present two children, one who is moving into silent reading, and one who is starting to read informational books.

Learning Silent Reading

Jake was working with his tutor, Pam. He was ready to make the transition to silent reading and they had begun to work on it. Jake was reading the book *Fox Outfoxed* (Marshall, 1992). They began the activity by looking through the book and remembering the part that Jake had already read. Jake read a page silently. Their routine was to work with troublesome words first. Jake mentioned that he had trouble with *gang* but just called it *guys* and that it made sense. Pam said that was fine and helped him sound out *gang*. Jake thought the word *costume* was *customers* so the sentence did not make sense to him. Pam asked him to think about what we know about the story, "What is it? What's going on here?"

> *Jake:*   Well, Halloween is coming and Fox and his gang and his friends were
>   excited and I thought it was *customers*. My customers will be really
>   wild. And then I thought it was talking about tricks to do on all of
>   them and the Fox says keep it down because I want...

134

Pam: Um hm (pause) This word is *costume.* 'Cause it's Halloween.

Notice she just told him the word. It was obvious that he had worked on it and had been unsuccessful. She also may have made the decision because she wanted to focus instruction on comprehension.

Jake: Costume, OK.

Pam: I want you...you just did a good job of telling me everything that happened on that page. So now I want you to tell me what you think about it. Tell me why.

Jake: It was a pretty good page.

Pam: You told me about. Now you said, "Let me show you." This is what I want you to do. [she read the page aloud] Fox and the gang were excited. "My costume will be really wild," said [unintelligable syllable]. "Think of all the tricks we can pull," said Dexter. "Keep your voices down," said Fox. "We don't want any little kids tagging along." Let me show you what I would want you to do. Well Fox and his friends are getting ready for Halloween and they are kind of excited about the, costumes are gonna be really wild and I forgot which one said be quiet because we don't want the little kids to come along. They think they are really cool 'cause they are older now and they want to go by themselves and they'll go scare people. Do you see how I told that back in my own words?

She had Jake read the next page out loud and retell it in his own words, which he did fairly well.

Pam: Oh, I liked the way you used your own words better that time. OK? Do you know why I'm having you put it in your own words? Do you know why I'm telling you that? Do you know why?

Jake: Because I'll understand it better.

Pam: Um hm. That's exactly right.

In this example, Pam was modeling and explaining thinking aloud. Jake was at a transition point and needed to focus his reading on comprehension.

135

Learning to Read Expository Texts

Mary was just beginning to read informational books and we were discussing how she decided what books to read. She had explained that she looked at the title and she read the back cover of the book and she tried a few pages. She had just pointed to a book to begin this conversation about informational books.

Cathy: You said, "these kinda books." What kind of books are these?

Mary: Yeah. It's like facts and stuff.

Cathy: Factual books?

Mary began reading the back cover and she had a lot of trouble with it.

Mary: (finishes reading) I think this is too hard for me.

Cathy: So what would you do?

Mary: I wouldn't read it.

Cathy: You wouldn't read it. If you really wanted to read it what would you do?

Mary: Well, look through it.

Cathy: OK. Like you...

Mary: Or have somebody else read it to me.

Cathy: You might have somebody else read it to you. That'd be a good strategy. Or sometimes if you pair with somebody you can help each other. Um, is there any. Um, one of the things that is true about a book like this is that you don't have to be able to read the whole thing to be able to read things that you are interested in. Um, like is there any particular animal that you'd like to know about?

Because Mary was making a transition, I was going to teach some strategies that she could use in reading informational prose. I wanted her to realize that you do not have to read a book from cover to cover if you just want to know particular information.

Mary: Ummm, monkeys (she turns to a section on Chimpanzees).

Cathy: Oh, you really like monkeys. I think this...chimpanzee. This is what this is. Now one thing you can do to get yourself ready, is start with the pictures. So what's going on in this picture?

Mary: They're in a tree.

Cathy: Um hm. And what does it say?

Mary: Chimpanzees live in groups.

We continued going through the pictures and reading the captions. Then I introduced a skimming strategy.

Cathy: OK. So one of the things you can do kind of is before you read you skim and see if there are any hard words. Don't read it.

Mary: In this one?

Cathy: Um hm, in *chimpanzee*. (pause) So are you finding some? (pause) What are you finding? Tell me about what you're doing.

Mary: Um, I'm looking and see if I find any hard words?

Cathy: Have you found any?

Mary: Two.

Cathy: Those two? Any more?

Mary: Is that *baboons*?

Cathy: It sure is. OK, so if you only find two hard words right off the bat, you might be able to read this part, huh? So that's one of the things you can do...is kind of look at a part and see, well, I wonder how many hard words this part has. OK, so now go ahead and read.

Mary read the entry and was able to figure out the difficult words on her own. We were running out of time and I wanted to emphasize comprehension, so I interrupted.

Cathy: OK, we're getting close. So let's stop here. Now can you sort of, in your own words, tell what that told you about chimpanzees. What did you learn about chimpanzees?

Mary: They live in groups and they live in different places. They live in tall grass and tropical rain forests and 20 to 40 chimpanzees and they eat ants (unintelligible) tail monkeys.

Cathy: So they eat a lot of different things. OK. So what do you think about this book? Could, how would you think about it?

Mary: It could be a "just right" book.

Cathy: Yeah it could. Parts of it could be just right and maybe if you were really interested in something you'd know enough about that topic that the words in that part of the book would be easy enough for you. And in your retelling, I think it showed that you did understand that part. So that's always the key. If you can understand it, then it's OK. OK? Thanks Mary.

In this reading my objective was to teach Mary some flexible strategies for working with informational texts. I suggested that she find a part she was interested in, explore the pictures first, skim for hard words, and then read. I had her check herself to see if she was understanding, and by the end of the lesson she realized that she would be able to read at least some of the parts of the book.

I began this chapter by covering some general principles for interacting with children during reading the new book. I stressed the importance of the book being at an appropriate difficulty level, and I talked about choice, wait time, when to teach, and encouraging children's use of multiple flexible strategies. Then I presented some examples of emergent, beginning, and transition readers as they read new books with their tutors. The emergent readers, Brandi and Ken demonstrated how emergent readers conceptions of reading need to be shaped and how book introductions help emergent readers read books they would otherwise be unable to read. The beginning reader, Tommie, demonstrated that the task for beginning readers is to coordinate all their knowledge, and the transition readers, Jake and Mary show how reading the new book shifts to a focus on silent reading, comprehension and learning new information. These examples are brief and cannot possibly teach all a tutor needs to know, but they do capture the ways reading the new book changes in response to the needs of the child.

FOR THE SUPERVISOR

This chapter is probably the most important chapter in the book. Reading the new book is the part of the lesson in which the child learns, and learns to apply, new strategies. It is important that you thoroughly discuss each of the examples in the chapter to make sure that tutors understand where a particular decision point is, what triggers that decision point, and why the particular decision is made. You should help the tutors understand for example, why I did not stop and correct Brandi when she was reading *comes* for *came*, but why I did talk with her about it afterward, and why I would not have talked at all to a transition reader who had called *came*, *comes*. How did I decide to ask Matt, "How did you know it was *after* and not *and*?" and why did

Jake's tutor just tell him the word *costume*? This chapter deserves ample attention in training sessions that should include time to talk about the examples that come up in the tutors' sessions with their children. You should provide help and guidance so that they will learn to make instructional decisions that are right for the child they are working with. When you are supervising you also should check to see that this segment of the lesson is taking about one third of the instructional time.

Chapter 10

Writing

As I *discuss in Chapter 6, writing and reading go together.* Writers compose messages and stories by deciding what they want to say and then using a writing system to put that message on paper. Their hope is that the reader of their writing will be able to interpret their intended message. Readers process written material as it appears on the page and try to determine this intended message. However, there is a sense in which reading and writing are so intertwined that it is not accurate to view them separately. As we move a message either toward the printed page by writing or away from the printed page by reading, we do many of the same things. In reading we must compose or construct the message. We must take the marks on the page, the letters, and turn them into words, sentences, paragraphs, and meaning. What is on the page serves as cues to readers and the readers must respond to those cues and create the message by reordering information in their minds. Reading one's own writing to check for the intended message also helps the writer to understand what he or she wants to say and in so doing prompts the writer to revise. Because there are many important overlapping features in the reading and writing process, practice and experience with either can help improve performance in the other.

THE WRITING PROCESS

Many of us think of writing as something that Writers with a capital *W* do. We admire the perfect prose we read in books, newspapers, and magazines, and we generally think that only a very elite group of people is capable of "real writing." In many of our daily lives there is little reason for us to write because we use other forms of communication such as the telephone to talk with one another. A legacy left over from schooling for many people is the belief that they cannot "really write." What we remember about writing is the papers returned to us with red corrections. Our papers, even if they looked neat when we turned them in, never came back looking as perfect as the published writing we read. The contrast between our writing and professional writing was great.

Donald Graves's 1983 book *Writing: Children and Teachers at Work* began to change many researchers' and teachers' notions of who writers are, how they write, and how writing should be taught. Graves encouraged educators to think of writing in school as a process similar to the one that professional writers use and thus to change the way writing was taught. He pointed out that real writers usually *choose* the topics they write about and that they often do not write in response to assignments. Their writing can be intensely personal and they generally write about something because they want to. Graves also pointed out that real writers do not write in a vacuum. They often read their writing to others, testing it to see how readers respond. When readers do not respond as they intended, they go back and rewrite and revise their writing. He noted that many writers pay little attention to mechanics and correctness when they are working on drafts because punctuation, spelling, and capitalization are simply not important in the early stages. Writers know that if they can get the message or the story down and make it work on readers the way the want it to work, they can edit it for correctness later. Furthermore, many of them will rely on editors to make sure the work is mechanically perfect. Real writers also spend large blocks of time on their writing—time that we rarely allow children in schools.

Graves's work has revolutionized the teaching of writing in many schools. Tutors will find that children in schools that use the process approach to teaching writing write a great deal and think of themselves as real writers. There are several basic concepts involved in using the process approach: choice, time, drafting, response, revising, editing, and publishing. What follows is a brief description of the writing process as developed by Graves and other proponents of process writing.

Choice

Probably the biggest problem most writers face is that they have nothing they want to say. How many of you after a routine summer during which you did nothing unusual, wrote *My Summer Vacation* at the top of the page and sat forever without writing because it seemed that nothing was worth telling? On the other hand, when I returned from Hilo, Hawaii after watching lava flow down a hillside and into the ocean, I was anxious to write about it because it was such an awesome sight. In her book *Radical Reflections* (1993), Mem Fox wrote that when we write we should "ache with caring." It is hard to ache with caring about a topic assigned by the teacher to the entire class. Choice therefore is one of the basic tenets of process writing. Because writing is hard work that may need to be taken through many revisions to achieve its intended goals, it is essential that writers, including child writers, care about what they write. Only intense caring can sustain the level of motivation necessary to produce powerful writing. For tutors, choice means giving the child time and space to discover a topic he or she really cares about. This means talking with the child, making lists, exploring books, or modeling your own choice of a topic—whatever it takes to help find the topic that makes him or her "ache with caring."

Time

Writers usually spend at least 3 or 4 concentrated hours per day on their writing. I try to set aside at least 2 days and hopefully 3 days a week when I can devote the late morning and early afternoon to writing. Not surprisingly, most of us do not feel like real writers because few among us can carve out that much time. Children in tutoring sessions are no exception. However, sometimes children will be in classrooms with teachers who use a process approach to organize their classrooms in writing workshops, and who set aside at least 45 minutes to an hour each day for the workshop on at least 3 days a week. Because the children know that they have specific time to write on a regular basis, they begin to see that they do have the time to write. When they have found something to write about (after choosing their own topic), they use that time to write. In this case the tutor can play the role of another adult helper working with the teacher to support the child through the writing process. If the child is not in a setting that allows time for writing the tutor can work with the child's parents or teacher to create such a setting. However, if this is not possible the tutor may have to restrict writing goals for tutoring sessions.

Drafting

Many of us, children included, get so worried about whether our writing is *correct* that we write in jerks and starts: We write a sentence, read it, decide it is not right, correct it, reread it, decide it still is not right, get discouraged, and quit. If we think of our early attempts as *drafts* rather than final products, we can short-circuit the correction cycle and let the words simply flow onto the page knowing that, if we like, we can make it perfect later. First drafts (sometimes even third and fourth drafts) are rarely perfect. They may contain spelling errors and sloppy punctuation. They may be unorganized and they may not say exactly what we want them to. But they are written; they do get the message on the page in some form, giving us raw material that we can shape into a final product. Drafting is sometimes difficult for tutors because although draft writing offers so many opportunities for teaching, it not a time for teaching. Instead, it is a time to encourage and support and stay out of the way because the point of drafting is to get ideas onto paper. I find that one of the best things to do while the child is drafting is to draft something myself. It provides a good model and keeps me out the child's way.

Response

One mistake many would-be writers make is believing that writing is done in isolation. Although some writers may work alone, most do not. At a minimum they have an ongoing dialogue with an editor, and most writers have a group of peers with whom they share their writing in its draft stages. For example, reading draft writing and sharing it with colleagues is one of the mainstays of the world-famous Iowa Writer's Workshop attended by many of our current contemporary writers including Kurt Vonnegut, Flannery O'Conner, John Irving, Jane Smiley, Wallace Stegner, and Sandra Cisneros. Sharing writing with a group you trust is necessary, especially for novices. You put words on the page intending a certain message, hoping for a certain response. When you share your writing, you actually hear the response of the reader and you can measure it against what you intended. Often writers find that the response they predicted did not happen perhaps because they left out important information or failed to make a point clearly. Or maybe an unexpected response to a particular detail encourages the writer to go back and tell more about that detail. Writers are frequently reluctant to revise what they have written if they feel that the writing says what they intended. It is only when there is a disparity between the writer's intention and the reader's interpretation that there is motivation for revision.

Responding to other people's writing is an art that must be taught. Writers can be fragile, especially if they are writing about something they care about. Comments about spelling and punctuation may damage their motivation and communicate only their lack of competence. Early response must be positive because a negative response can kill writing before it is really written.

Good early response is based on careful attention to the writing. If you like something, tell the child specifically what you like using the words he or she wrote. If you have questions, ask them. Often a writer does not know what a potential audience knows. Your questions can suggest information that will be interesting and useful to the reader. In early stages however, you must be very careful with suggestions. Remember the writing belongs to the child, not to you. Suggestions must provide an opportunity for the child to consider or reject them.

Revision

Revision is the hard work of writing. It is not, as is commonly assumed, simply checking for mechanics or correctness; that is editing, which I will talk about next. When we revise we try to make our message clear. Often revising involves reorganizing what we say so it comes in an order that helps the reader best comprehend our intended message. Revising also involves adding information where response (from peers with whom we have shared the piece) indicated that it was lacking. It sometimes means deleting unnecessary detail where response indicated redundancy or rewording sentences to make them say more precisely what we mean. It may mean checking for voice—is the style consistent? If it is inconsistent, is there a reason for the inconsistency? Or should it be changed?

Revising is hard work and it is often very difficult to get children, or even adult writers, to revise. The only reason to revise is to make the message clear to the reader. If there is no real reader, as is often the case with school assignments, revising makes very little sense. The most important thing a tutor can do to encourage revision is to make sure that the writing is done for a real audience. A story that will be read by the tutor and stuck in a folder does not merit revision. A story that will be included in a class or program anthology and distributed to students, read during school assembly, or printed in a student paper will probably merit revision. The tutor must work hard to capture real audiences for the child's writing.

Editing

Editing is what we do to ready a piece for publishing. It is concerned mainly with clarity, mechanics, and correctness. The writing process approach encourages us to make editing the final stage of writing. To be sure, writers do edit their own pieces.

When writers "ache with caring" about their topics, they want everything to be *right*. They do not want misspellings and incorrect punctuation to disrupt their message or cause the reader to dismiss the writing as insignificant because the writer clearly did not care enough to make it right. As writers develop, the sophistication of their editing develops as well. Young children may simply attend to punctuation and spelling. More sophisticated writers will check voice, tense, grammar, pronoun referents, and subject-verb agreement. Professional editors have checklists of items for editing. It is important to remember that professional writers work with an editor, sometimes several editors, at different stages of the writing process. They have copy editors and proofreaders at their disposal. Children also need access to good editors and proofreaders when they are publishing their writing. Tutoring is an excellent setting for editing because a more skilled adult whose job is to help the child is always available. However, the temptation can then be to focus only on editing in the tutoring session. Remember, editing is the last step and children must be given the freedom and trust to reach it.

A Caution

The brevity and list-like nature of the earlier explanation may convey the impression that the writing process is linear. It is most assuredly *not* linear. A writer may choose a topic, write a draft, abandon it and choose another topic, write a draft, gather response, revise, and then return to the first piece, returning later to the second piece. Or a writer may write a complete draft and gather response once, revise, edit, and publish. Another piece may be written in dribs and drabs, responded to many times, and taken through many revisions. One of the most inappropriate applications of process writing is to work step by step according to predetermined plan. Having the child choose a topic and draft on Monday, gather response on Tuesday, revise on Wednesday, edit on Thursday, and publish on Friday violates the basic assumptions of the writing process—that it is an individual act that is motivated by the "ache of caring." Tutors must be patient and in Graves's (1983) words, "lead from behind," allowing the child to direct the process and knowing when to encourage, when to help, and when to stay out of the way.

EMERGENT READERS

Writing is particularly important for emergent readers. Early writing helps children to understand the world of print by enabling their discovery that writing is a message and that it carries important meaning. Early writing also helps children develop an awareness that words are composed of sounds. For example, the word *that* is composed of three sounds: /th/, /a/, and /t/. This awareness of sounds in words called phonemic awareness is one of the most important predictors of reading difficulty. Children who begin first grade without this understanding are at high risk for reading failure. Although phonemic awareness can be taught in several ways (some of which I will talk about in Chapter 11), writing is one of the most natural places for its discovery. As I noted in Chapter 3, children who are encouraged to write soon begin to use letters to represent sounds. For example, children sometimes write *hkn* for *chicken* because they hear the /ch/ sound in *chicken* as they say the name of the letter *H*. This very early use of letter names to determine which letters appear in words indicates the child's understanding that words are made up of sounds that can be represented by letters—this shows phonemic awareness. Allowing children to use invented spellings in the emergent stages of reading and writing can increase this awareness. For example, when we say a word slowly and encourage the child to write down all the sounds he or she hears, we are assuming phonemic awareness. Each time we model this process for the child we are helping to teach it. Once the child realizes that words can be written by saying them slowly and listening for the letters, he or she can discover that thinking about the sounds of the letters can help in reading words.

The type of writing activities included in your tutoring sessions will depend on how much time you have. If you have a 45-minute to 1-hour session, it is possible to actually have the child write his or her own pieces and use the principles of the writing process to help the child move from topic choice to publication (at least on some pieces). If you have only a half hour you may want to restrict the goals for writing. If the child is involved in an active writing workshop in his or her classroom, you may be able to support the child wherever in the process his or her present piece is located. However, if the child's school or home settings do not encourage much writing, you might have the child write a single sentence and use the writing of that sentence to teach about letter-sound correspondences.

For example, suppose you have just completed the reading of a story and you ask the child to give you a sentence that tells something about the story. The child says, "I think the lady is silly to give the animals a bath." How you proceed with the sentence will depend on what the child knows. Let us assume that the words *I*, *the*, *is*, *to*, and *a* are in the child's writing vocabulary. You have the child write *I* and then you ask the child what sounds he or she hears *think* because you know that the child is familiar with the /th/ correspondence and knows the sounds of *i*, *n*, and *k*. You may have the child write first on scratch paper or a practice sheet before writing the complete sentence correctly. Suppose the child writes *th i k*. Once again what you do will be influenced by what the child knows. If the child has done little work with blends, you might simply say, "Very good, you got four of the five sounds! But listen to me as I say the end of the word slowly, *thhhhhiiiiiiiinnnnnnnkkkkk*. Do you hear the *n* sound right before the *k*? Put it in there." Have the child write the word correctly in his or her notebook. If however, you have been working on blends in general, or on the /nk/ blend in particular, you should let the child do much more of the work. For example, you might say, "Very good. You got four of the five sounds. Say that word slowly and really listen at the end." If the child were successful, he or she would write the word. If not, you might try pronouncing *thick* and *think* to call attention to /nk/ blend. In any event, the writing of the sentence can become a very important place for teaching letter-sound relations.

BEGINNING READERS

Writing is also useful for beginning readers who are expanding their repertoires and writing longer, more sophisticated pieces. As a tutor you always should focus on the message of the child's writing first. Once the tutor has responded to content, the child can continue to use the writing exercise as a time to learn and reinforce letter-sound relations. Writing also can be used to reinforce the learning of sight vocabulary.

Struggling readers often have two kinds of problems. First, they often cannot use letter-sound relations to figure out a word. Second, once they have figured out the word, they do not remember it the next time they see it. One of the most frustrating discoveries about reading difficulty is how hard it can be for some children to remember words. Although the precocious reader remembers every word after only one exposure, some struggling readers will not remember a word after 70 or more exposures. Learning to write and spell can help these children remember. Building a basic sight vocabulary is one of the major tasks of the beginning reading stage and using writing to help them learn that vocabulary is an important strategy for sight-vocabulary learning.

Once again writing activities will be dictated by the length of the tutoring sessions. If you have ample time, include the entire writing cycle. When you edit, focus on critical letter-sound relations and target high-frequency vocabulary for learning. You may want to supply some sort of reference point for the child who simply cannot remember how to spell words such as *what, here, where,* and *were.* Classroom teachers sometimes use a word wall—they write words on tag board and stick them to the wall, usually organizing the words alphabetically under their initial letters. In tutoring, a word bank (a box with the words on individual cards) or a simple pamphlet that has a letter of the alphabet at the top of each page can be very helpful. The child records words starting with that letter on each page. Sometimes drawing a quick sketch beside the word to serve as a clue to help identify the word will help the child use the booklet.

If your time is limited, the writing of a single sentence or two or three sentences as I described in the section on emergent readers can be very beneficial. Again, when you are writing, focus first on the message or content and then concentrate on critical letter-sound relations and target frequently occurring sight vocabulary.

TRANSITION READERS

In the transition stage readers are beginning to explore the various genres of writing. They are learning to read informational as well as narrative prose and they may study more poetry, biography, and historical prose. Reading and writing demands are particularly significant in the area of informational prose. Several new types of organization including general-specific, cause-effect, and problem-solution appear, making special demands on the reader. Take for example, the general-specific organization of the paragraph that I used on page 26 in Chapter 2:

> Birds build nests in many places. Eagles build nests on cliffs. Robins build nest in trees. Pheasants build nests on the ground. Pheasants have beautiful feathers.

Children include sentences like "Pheasants have beautiful feathers" in their paragraphs and need help to see why they do not belong. Recall also the child's piece about kangaroos on page 95 in Chapter 6. There is a sense of randomness about the facts the child included in her story, and a mixture of a chronological and more factual style. In revision a tutor might make suggestions about categories of information that she could put in a series of paragraphs—categories such as physical appearance, social characteristics, and reproduction. We might show her some descriptions of animals in an encyclopedia, children's magazine, or dictionary. As she learns about the expository format in writing, she will develop the necessary knowledge and strategies needed for understanding prose written in this format.

FOR THE SUPERVISOR

The most difficult task for tutors is determining what part of a piece of writing they should focus on with the student. They often forget to attend to the child's message and thus convey that writing is an exercise for learning to read and not something the child can use to communicate his or her thoughts and feelings. Supervisors will want to remind tutors consistently that it is the message of the writing that is most important and that they can convey that importance by responding to content first.

Tutors also have a tendency to teach everything that comes up as it comes up. They may not have a good sense of what the child knows and what the child might learn next. For example, in the emergent section I gave the example of teaching the /nk/ in *think*. Tutors often assume that because the child knows both the /n/ and /k/ sounds, combining the two will not be a problem. However, because the /n/ is a sound that is produced in the nasal passage, it is difficult to hear, particularly in the middle of a word next to other consonants. Tutors often will need help to decide when to teach strategies like this. If they do not recognize the difficulty of /n/ blends and many other blends, they will teach this exercise too early. It is here that you can be of the most use. You need to help tutors identify the sounds the child knows and help them understand a logical sequence for teaching whatever comes next. There are several good sources for gathering this kind of information. I recommend *Phonics for Teachers of Reading* (Hull & Fox, 1997). The tutors of beginning readers need help in keeping track of sight vocabulary and more complicated letter-sound relations. Any basic reading methods text contains these lists. I recommend *Reading as Communication* (May, 1997). Tutors of transition readers need help in understanding how the concept of genre develops in young readers and writers. In addition to Graves's work discussed earlier in the chapter, *The Art of Teaching Writing* (Calkins, 1994) is another useful source for information about teaching writing.

Chapter 11

Minilessons

I USUALLY *think of minilessons as a strategy to use with a whole class or small group.* I have used the term here, however, because I like its emphasis on short length. Mini-lessons suggest abbreviated lessons conducted in response to children's *observed* needs. They do not appear at a particular place in some predetermined scope and sequence skills chart. In this first example, I hope to explain why and how you would teach a specific minilesson in a tutoring session by showing how a lesson event suggests a possible minilesson.

LESSONS SUGGEST MINILESSONS

Manny and I were reading the book *Horace*. The text read *"No, Horace, you can't come," said Dad. So Horace howled.* Manny read fluently until he got to the word *howled.* He hesitated for a long time and guessed, "had?"

I said, "OK, it has to be a noise he's making."

"Howled?"

"Um hm. Did you see how I did that?"

"No."

"I looked at Horace and Dad, and Dad just told him he couldn't come. So I was thinking about the meaning. And then I thought, 'Well, what could start with *h?*'"

I was doing some incidental teaching about using meaning and initial consonants to help with word identification. However, I taught it on the fly and I was not really satisfied that Manny understood. I am not sure a young reader could figure out that it was a noise just from the context, so in some ways my, "OK. It has to be a noise," was not a good cue. You would have to be able to read the word to know it was a noise and that would not help the child if he were on his own. I needed to provide cues that the child could use when I was not there.

It is sometimes hard to be as explicit and as accurate as you need to be when you are teaching incidentally. Because using meaning and initial consonants together was an important goal for Manny that had presented problems in the example above and fairly consistently throughout his lessons, it made sense to follow up with a minilesson.

My minilessons usually include the initial steps of direct instruction. Many models for direct instruction exist but I use one (loosely derived from Hunter, 1976) that includes six components. These components do not necessarily occur in sequential order. The components include (1) introduction, (2) modeling and explanation, (3) feedback, (4) guided practice, (5) independent practice, and (6) evaluation. In minilessons I usually include the first three steps. I do the last three steps as the child reads in the new-book segments and sometimes in the challenge-book segments of the tutoring session. (Chapter 6 in *Variability Not Disability* also addresses the topic of minilessons.)

Table 12 contains a dialogue that might occur if I followed up the interaction with Manny with a minilesson. Notice that it allows me to go back and model more explicitly and accurately the processes a reader might use. What I will do in the remaining sections of this chapter is give an example of a minilesson that might be appropriate for a child at each stage of reading development and provide a list of minilessons that might be taught. It should be clear from the examples that minilessons come *out of instruction* and not *off a list*. I include the lists here only to help you think about the kinds of things children might need to learn. The lists are not exhaustive and they are not in any specific sequence. They should not be used like a scope and sequence chart (a curriculum plan in which the objectives or skills are organized according to the levels at which they are taught). Marching through the lessons on the lists will not turn children into readers. You must look at what a particular child is doing in order to decide what you should teach in a minilesson.

Table 12
Emergent Reader Minilesson for Using Meaning
Plus Initial Consonants in Word Identification

Introduction	Remember yesterday when we were reading *Horace?* You read, "'No, Horace, you can't come,' said Dad. So Horace..." You didn't know what the next word was, so I helped you and then you knew that word was *howled.* What I want to do now is explain how you can use the meaning of the story that you understand so far to help you figure out that word.
Modeling and Explanation	First, when we introduced the book, you noticed that Horace wants to do things with all these people and he is not very happy because they won't let him. So you read, "No, Horace you can't come," said Dad. So Horace..." and you were stuck on the word (point to *howled* written on the dry-erase board). Now let's think about this. Horace's dad just told him he can't go. Horace is probably pretty unhappy. And the book says, *So Horace....* The way that sentence is going, it is probably something Horace did. What could he do that shows he is unhappy and that begins with the /h/ sound? And when you think about meaning and use your sounds, it will help you say the words. Now today as you are reading your new book if you come to a word you're not sure of, I want you to think about the meaning so far and think about the sounds and see if that helps you.
Feedback	What do I want you to do? Hopefully the child will be able to give a brief explanation of what you want him or her to do.

EMERGENT READER

In the lesson described earlier, Manny was an emergent reader. Another example from this stage shows Danny learning to make a word-print match. He was reading a highly patterned book about where animals live. On each page the sentence said, A _____ *lives in a* _____. Danny read quite fluently and named each animal and each home, but on the third page he began adding *and* at the beginning of each sentence. It was obvious that he was not making a complete word-print match. He may have been simply repeating the pattern and using the pictures to fill in the animal and the home. This kind of approximation of reading is appropriate for early emergent readers, although once they begin to have some sight vocabulary, they can begin to match the word and the print. Danny knew the words *in*, *a*, and *and*, as well as about 25 other basic words. It was appropriate for him to be making the word-print match. His tutor asked him to point to the words as he said them, and he realized that there were not enough words on the page to match the sentences he was saying, "And a rabbit lives in a hole." He then went back and carefully read the sentence to match the print. Table 13 presents a possible minilesson for Danny, and Table 14 is a list of possible minilessons for this stage. Remember they are not in any specific order and they do not represent all the possible minilessons that you could teach.

Table 13 **Emergent Reader Minilesson for Matching Word and Print**	
Introduction	Remember yesterday when we were reading the book about animals' homes? You were reading it really well and I asked you to point to the words on the page about the rabbit. When you pointed you ran out of words to point to. So you went back and looked carefully at the words and you realized that it didn't say, *And the rabbit lives in a hole.* It said, *The rabbit lives in a hole.* Today I want you to point to the words on the page to make sure that what you say matches what the book says.
Modeling and Explanation	We also had trouble at the end of that book on the spider page. You read that page, "A spider lives in a web." But the book said this, (point to *Who lives in the web? A spider* written on a dry-erase board). Now look. Let's point as I say what you read. Oops! There are words left over, aren't there? So let's look really closely and see if we can figure it out. That first word isn't *a*, I don't think you know that word; it's *who*. So point to *who* and then see if you can read the page and make what you say match the print. Now today when we read our new book I want you to point to the words and make what you say match what the print says.
Feedback	What do I want you to do today when we read the new book? Hopefully the child will give a brief explanation of what you want him or her to do.

Table 14
Some Possible Minilessons for Emergent Readers

- You read books from the top to the bottom.
- The print goes from the left to the right.
- The front of the book has the title and author.
- The words are made up of sounds.
- The words must make sense.
- The words often go with the pictures on the page.
- Words that look alike often sound alike. (*fine-pine*; *began-before*)
- A word often looks the same each time it is on the page.
- Sometimes words look a little different on the page. (*the-The*)
- A particular letter makes a particular sound. (This should be restricted to consonant sounds because they are fairly consistent.)
- Sometimes parts of words like *-ing* and *-ed* are the same. (play*ing*-go*ing*)
- Words that start with the same letter often start with the same sound. (*big-bit*)
- Words with ends that look alike also sound alike (*rain-pain*).
- You can write words by listening to the sounds as you say them.
- Stories make sense. Something happens to someone and it works out.
- You can make lists of words to help you remember things.
- You can leave notes when you will not see the person.
- Newspapers can tell us what happens in the world.
- Menus tell the choices of what to eat.

BEGINNING READERS

Beginning readers have a fairly good sense of what reading is and they understand a lot about many of the features of text and language that go into stories and reading. Their most basic task is to put all their knowledge together and make reading make sense. As I described in Chapter 9, Tommie was reading *Sheep in a Jeep*. We had talked a little about the book and then he read to me, "Beep, beep, beep. Sheep in a jeep on a hill that's sheep. Oh /s/ slip." The final word of the sentence was actually *steep*. After trying, Tommie looked at me and I said, "How is that word different from *sheep*?" He answered pointing to the specific letters, "Because that's a *h* and that's a *t*." "OK. Can you take the *sh* off and put the *st* on?" Tommie tried making the sounds of *s* and *t* but was getting nowhere, so I said, "And think about a hill.

What can a hill be?" Tommie immediately got steep and I commented that thinking about meaning can really help you when sounding is not doing very well.

Tommie was like many struggling readers that I have known. He had developed the habit of trying to sound out all words. He would keep trying sounds until someone helped—usually by saying the word for him. I wanted him to learn to use several methods to help him with unknown words. Table 15 contains a minilesson that might be appropriate for Tommie, and Table 16 has a list of minilessons appropriate for beginning readers.

Table 15
Beginning Reader Minilesson for Using Meaning
Plus Sounding Out

Introduction	Remember yesterday when we were reading *Sheep in a Jeep*? You were having trouble with the word (point to *steep* on the dry-erase board). You were trying to sound it out, but you weren't having much luck. Then I told you to think about the meaning of the sentence, *Beep, beep, beep. Sheep in a jeep on a hill that's….* And I said to think about the hill and ask what a hill could be. As soon as I said that, you knew that the word was *steep*. Thinking about the meaning can help you when sounding out isn't working for you. That's what I want to show you today.
Modeling and Explanation	I think I saw you use the meaning later on in that book. You were reading the sentences, "Oh ho, the jeep won't go. Sheep…" and the next word was (point to *leap* on the dry-erase board). First you said *jeep* and then *lamp*. Now lamp was a reasonable try because it does match the beginning and ending letters, but it didn't make sense. So you went back and said, "/l/, *leap*." *Leap* matches and it is something sheep could do. It made sense. You finished the sentence, "leap to push the jeep." You used the sounds but you made it make sense. That's what reading is all about—making sense. Today when you read your new book, remember that if sounding out isn't working, thinking about the meaning may help.
Feedback	What do I want you to do today when we read the new book? Hopefully the child will give a brief explanation of what you want him or her to do.

Table 16
Some Possible Minilessons for Beginning Readers

- Reading must make sense.
- Making a picture in your head of what is happening can help you understand.
- Stories make sense. Something happens to someone and it works out.
- Stories have beginnings, middles, and ends.
- Stories can be realistic or they can be imagined.
- Skipping ahead and returning to hard words can help you figure them out.
- Rereading something can help you read better.
- If one thing is not working on a word, try something else.
- Words that have -igh in them sound like the /I/ in Hi. (Teach other common word patterns.)
- -tion says shun. (Teach other common suffixes.)
- Relating what you know to the book can help you understand.
- Predicting what will come next will help you understand.
- Trying to understand why the author said something can help you understand.
- Looking for common prefixes and suffixes can help you figure out words.
- Looking for common root words can help you understand and pronounce words.
- Dividing words into smaller parts can help you pronounce them.
- Reading several books about the same thing can help you learn special words.
- A dictionary can help you with word meanings.
- A dictionary can help you with word pronunciations.

TRANSITION READERS

Minilessons for transition readers emphasize ways to make meaning from text and teach comprehension strategies. For example, remember Trevor, the transition reader (see Chapter 1 page 17) who was learning to think aloud about text. As I worked with him I noticed that when he stopped to tell me about the story he seemed to trying to reproduce the page verbatim. During the lessons I gave him the following instruction:

> OK now, when you tell me what's on the page you don't have to tell me every word exactly what's on the page. You can kinda interpret it yourself. Like if I were telling you about this, what I would say is, "Um, the little girl ran in and told her parents about the beaver, and then Mom and Dad kind of thought about everything and they remembered the bark, sticks, and the branches, and they decided that there must be beavers building a lodge." So you don't have to just give every word, you just have to think about it and tell what it means to you.

Trevor was like many transition readers who have struggled to learn to read. He had somehow developed the conception of reading as repeating what you have read. I'm not sure how this happened for Trevor, but it may have happened because his reading instruction had focused only on pronouncing words and answering very

---

Table 17
Transition Reader Minilesson for Thinking Aloud

Introduction	Yesterday when we were reading, I asked you stop after reading and talk about what you reading. The first couple times you tried to tell me everything that was on the page. But I told you I didn't want you to tell me everything. Do you remember? [Hopefully he does.] Today I want to teach you something I call thinking aloud. When you read, as you come to the end of each sentence, you stop and think aloud. You stop and tell me what it means, what you are thinking.
Modeling and Explanation	I have a text here about seven blind mice. It begins, "One day seven blind mice were surprised to find a strange Something by their pond. "What is it?" they cried, and they all ran home" Now let me show you what I'm thinking. "Hmmm. This story is going to be interesting. I wonder how blind mice are going to figure out what it is. Let's read the next page. "On Monday, Red Mouse went first to find out." Oh, I bet this is going to be a week of the day book. That's probably why there are seven mice. I wonder why there are only six mice in the picture. There's green, yellow, purple, red, blue, and white. Wait there are seven. Red mouse is on the other page. That must must be orange. I think I know what the something is going to be. That looks like an elephant's leg. Let's read the next page. "It's a pillar," he said. And no one believed him." Oh. This story is going to be like the story of the six blind men from India. Now let's read the next page and you try. [The lessons would continue with the child and I alternating turns until I was confident that the child understood the task.]
Feedback	Today when we read we're going to think aloud. What will I want you to do when we stop? Hopefully the child will give a correct explanation.

Based on Young, E. (1992). *Seven Blind Mice*. New York: Philomel Books.

literal questions. Or it may have happened because Trevor had been tested frequently with IRIs that require retellings. Both of these explanations fit many transition readers. Table 17 is a minilesson about thinking aloud. Also, in minilessons with transition readers, I sometimes use examples from my own reading. Table 18 is a minilesson based on my reading of Wallace Stegner's *Shooting Star*, and Table 19 is a list of minilessons for transition readers.

Table 18 Transition Reader Minilesson for Fixing Comprehension Problems	
Introduction	Sometimes when you are reading, things don't quite make sense. Can you think of a time when something didn't make sense to you? (Be sure to get at least one example from the child.) Today we're going to talk about what to do when things don't make sense.
Modeling and Explanation	The other day I was reading a novel about a family and a guest watching meteor showers. Leonard, the father, had finished doing the dishes, so he arrived late. When he got to the backyard, the mother and one daughter were lying on a blanket and the guest and the other daughter were sitting on lounge chairs. The children began arguing about how many falling stars they had seen. And the text said, *He groaned down exaggeratedly weary, and they made room. They lay four in a row on the blanket. Four in a row on the blanket* stopped me. By my calculations it should be three. Leonard, the mother, and one daughter. I went back and reread and realized that I had missed the sentence, *Louise left her chair by Sabrina and flopped down.* When I reread I realized that the mother and the two daughters were on the blanket so that when the father sat down there were four on the blanket. One of the first things to do when your reading isn't making sense is to go back and reread.
Feedback	What do I want you to do today when we read the new book? Hopefully the child will give a brief explanation of what you want him or her to do.
Stegner, W. (1961). *Shooting Star* (pp. 247–248). New York: Penguin Books.	

Table 19
Some Possible Minilessons for Transition Readers

- Reading must make sense.
- Making a picture in your head of what is happening can help you understand.
- Stories have settings, characters, plots, endings, and themes.
- Stories can be realistic or they can be imagined.
- Books can be informational.
- Paragraphs in informational books may use a pattern of organization such as general/specific, cause/effect, chronological, problem solution, or spatial.
- Rereading something helps you understand it.
- If one thing is not solving your problem, try something else.
- Roots from Latin, French, and German can help build your vocabulary
- Relating what you know to the book can help you understand it.
- Predicting what will come next will help you understand the text.
- Summarizing what a paragraph, section, or chapter has said can help you understand and remember.
- Trying to understand why the author said something can help you understand the book.
- Looking for common root words can help you understand and pronounce words.
- Reading several books about the same thing can help you learn special words.
- A dictionary can help you with word meanings.
- A dictionary can help you with word pronunciations.
- Talking with a friend about what you read can help you understand it.
- Taking notes on a text can help you understand and remember it.

FOR THE SUPERVISOR

Tutors will need a lot of help choosing minilessons. While emphasizing that minilessons must grow out of instruction, you must help them see which one of several to many possibilities is the best minilesson to teach. Choosing the best lesson depends on knowing well both what the child knows and what the normal sequences of development are. Although Chapter 3 will help in this area, it is unreasonable to expect that a single chapter can provide tutors with everything they need to know.

The tutors need to know how knowledge of letters and sounds develop for emergent and beginning readers. They need to remember that consonant sounds are fairly reliable and that vowel sounds are much less predictable. You may want to remind them of the chart of phonograms on page 51. For those students who have had little exposure to phonics I recommend *Phonics for the Teacher of Reading* (Hull & Fox, 1997). It also may be helpful to review steps for teaching letter-sound relations and steps for teaching sight vocabulary. These are presented in most basic reading methods texts and I recommend the treatment in *Reading as Communication* (May, 1997).

For transition readers, tutors may need additional information about such things as word analysis; Greek, Latin, and English prefixes, suffixes, and root words; pronunciation keys; analysis of multisyllabic words; comprehension strategies; and characteristics of expository, narrative, and persuasive writing, poetry, and other genres. Again these are presented in most basic reading methods texts; May's treatments in *Reading as Communication* are also excellent.

Chapter 12

Reading Challenging Books

UNFORTUNATELY, FOR *many struggling readers there are very few or no books that they both want to and can read.* Throughout my career I have emphasized the importance of children reading in appropriately leveled materials—in texts that they can read with 90% to 95% accuracy. However, over the years I also have become convinced of the importance of children reading books they want to read—**even if they cannot read at high-accuracy levels.** Learning to read requires both sustained motivation and growing competence. Children need to read all levels of books, easy or vacation, just right, and dream or challenge (what educators traditionally refer to as independent, instructional, and frustration levels). They need to maintain a balance of levels. Easy books build confidence and develop fluency, just-right books provide optimal opportunities for learning reading strategies, and challenge books keep the child trying. Although I want to make very sure that children are spending at least 20 to 30 minutes reading easy and just-right books daily, I also want them to have *some* time to spend with challenging books.

MAKING CHALLENGING BOOKS ACCESSIBLE

In Chapter 4 of *Variability Not Disability*, Linda Fielding and I summarize ways to make challenging or difficult books accessible to struggling readers. These strategies include reading to children, partner reading, rereading, preceding difficult books with easier ones, and listening to taped books. As technology becomes more and more available we also can provide children with machines that will read books to them. It is now possible to place a book on a scanner and have a computer read the text aloud; when it comes to an unknown word it spells the word. Such technology is available in some reading clinics and special settings.

Tutoring is an ideal setting for reading challenging books because the tutor is there to provide help as it is needed. It is important for children to understand that the tutor provides different kinds of help with different kinds of books. In easy books children need little help and can read on their own. The point of easy reading is to provide practice, build fluency, and enjoy the book. Children should know that you will not provide a lot of instruction during easy reading. On the other hand, reading the new book is a time when children should expect to use, practice, and be taught reading strategies. They should understand that this is a time when they work at learning to read. In challenging books children should know that you will help when help is needed. Otherwise the reading experience will be unpleasant.

When I work with children in tutoring sessions I clearly label each book and remind the child of the level of support that I will provide. I may say, "This is our easy book, the one you can read all by yourself," or "This is our just-right book. You can do most of this on your own, but you may need help in a few places," or "This is the challenge book. It may be hard for you and I will help you when you need help."

In Chapter 1, I noted that there are many ways to share the reading task and that tutors, parents, and teachers often discover these on their own. The simplest way to take turns is to have the adult read the entire book and then have the child read it. Sometimes the child and the tutor alternate turns with words or phrases, sentences, paragraphs, or pages. In many ways reading challenging books is the same in every stage of reading because by definition a challenging book is one the child needs a lot of help with. In the examples that follow of an emergent, beginning, and transition reader, I use several patterns of turn taking, some of which may appear in one stage and not in another. Remember, however, that each of the patterns could appear in any of the stages; the examples of turn taking thus apply to all of the stages.

EMERGENT READER

I read with Alan for 6 intermittent weeks during the spring and summer of 1997. Alan was just completing first grade. His family and his teacher were concerned that his progress in learning to read was slow. In spring assessments he recognized only about 13 words on a 100-word list and he could not read a preprimer text with 90% to 95% accuracy. Alan was a very smart young boy however, and his thinking ability stretched far beyond the books he could actually read. He was very frustrated when he could not read what he knew were very simple books. We used several strategies to read these simple books, which for Alan, were challenging.

The first strategy was for Alan and I to read the sentence together and then have Alan read the same sentence by himself. Early on we read *Watching Foxes* (Arnosky, 1985). It is a book that for the most part has one sentence per page. The illustrations are beautiful and provide strong cues for word identification. Because the book was well beyond Alan's competence and because he was unusually uncooperative that day, I asked him to read it with me. By this I meant that I would read slowly and Alan would try to read the words with me. On most pages Alan could say at least a few of the words with me, and on some pages he could read most of them. Often times when I began the sentence Alan did not read and I would need to prompt him by saying, "read it with me." After we read the sentence together, I asked Alan to read it by himself. He often repeated the sentence without following the print so I asked him to read it again, "and point with your finger."

When we came to the page, *Mother comes back home*, I asked Alan if he could do this one on his own. He could and did. Alan chose this book on two more occasions; on his final reading, he read with 97% meaningful accuracy and we had delightful conversations about the story and illustrations. For example, Alan speculated on whether the baby foxes' claws could kill the pesky flea and wondered whether the claws would injure their ears.

A second pattern we used was for me to provide difficult words on some pages and to take over all the reading on others. In our last session together Alan and I read *Today I Think I'll Run Away* (Johnson, 1985). This is a patterned book about a little boy who runs away and encounters various demons and monsters. As he meets each one he takes something from his bag of cherished belongings and throws it to the ground. When he does, some natural obstacle appears that stops the monster but not the boy. Over the course of the book he meets a series of monsters including an ogre, a dragon, a demon, and a monster. The text for the opening pages reads as follows (italics added):

> Today I thought I'd run away. So I went upstairs and got my bag and *packed* it with my *special things, and* set *out.*

163

I hadn't gone very far when I met a *grumbling, rumbling, lumbering ogre.* So I *opened* my bag and took out my [good] comb and *threw* it on the ground and *made a forest grow.* It *was* too *thick* for the ogre, but I ran through it and *left* him behind.

The text from *I hadn't gone very far...* to left *him behind* is the pattern that repeats for each monster. The italicized words in the excerpt are the words that I pronounced for Alan, and he inserted *good* before *comb.* Although the story clearly was a challenge, Alan was able to read many of the words independently. When Alan finished this segment, he said, "Too thick for the ogre. I wonder what he means by that?" and we had a short discussion of how close together the trees in the forest were. Then I read the next sequence from *I hadn't gone very far....* to left *him behind.* And I read the dragon sequence through *...a hissing, spitting, sizzling.* Alan took over with the dragon and read fairly fluently needing help only with *my, belt, river, flow, wet,* and *across.* Because his reading of the phrase, *and made a river flow* was rather choppy, I repeated the phrase for him. I read the next sequence and Alan read the one that followed; we continued alternating turns and I occasionally helped with words and repeated phrases Allan struggled with. I consistently read the three participles and the noun that introduced each of the monsters. As we approached the end and the boy returned home, Alan said, "I thought he was going to run away?" and when he read the final lines, "I think I'll run away again...tomorrow," he laughed.

A final pattern I used with Alan was simply to help with difficult words as he needed it. Alan also read the book *Harbor* (Crews, 1982). This was his favorite book. He was very interested in boats and his family owned one that they used for recreation. During his initial reading of *Harbor* he needed help with most of the content words and many of the common sight words, and he still needed a lot of help on his second and third readings. But Alan loved *Harbor.* He looked at illustrations carefully and talked at length about how neat it was that the ferry did not have to turn around. He examined the details of the illustrations and when they did not match his expectations we had lengthy discussions to make sense of them. After his second reading, Alan chose *Harbor* every time I gave him a choice and ultimately read the book 10 times. He sometimes read the final pages without looking at the print and I reminded him to go back and read with the words.

These three examples of reading with Alan demonstrate three different patterns of reading the challenging book. First I read each sentence either with or to Alan and then he read the sentence after me. Second, I helped him with difficult words on an "as needed" basis and occasionally took over entire sequences to give Alan a break and keep the session moving forward. Third, I provided help with difficult words.

Alan's interest in and repeated readings of the final book allowed him to achieve a fluent and accurate reading all by himself.

Beginning Reader

During the spring and summer that I read with Alan, I also read with Keith, another child who was finishing first grade and whose parents and teachers were concerned about his reading progress. When we began instruction Keith had acquired a fairly large sight vocabulary and knew 97 of 100 words on a sight-word list. He could read simple texts independently at the primer level. On several occasions the boys chose to read the same challenge books and it is interesting to note how the support I offered the two boys differed. Keith chose *Watching Foxes* in the opening weeks of our sessions and read the book four times. On his first reading, I had Keith read the book independently, and he read with 86% meaningful accuracy. He needed help with words like *wake, flea, tasty, chew, pounces, ear,* and *tail.* I supported Keith by providing the words he could not identify easily which, in general was the level of support he needed. As a beginning reader Keith's knowledge of common sight words was fairly accurate and this knowledge in combination with strong picture cues was usually enough to allow him to read 80% to 85% of the words independently. With my support he could achieve a 90% to 95% accuracy level.

Keith also read *Today I Thought I'd Run Away.* On the day he first chose this book, we had difficult time. Although Keith was usually cooperative, on this day he was tired and had argued with his mother about coming to the session. He yawned and stalled and was anxious for the session to be over. By the time we got to the challenge book, we had both had it, and I simply read the book to him. We had a good interaction around the book and Keith enjoyed it. He laughed at the ending as Alan had.

Keith's second and last reading of the book occurred several weeks later on our last day of tutoring. He selected the book but had difficulty with the title and he asked if he had to read it. I read the title for him, *Today I Thought I'd Run Away.* Anticipating that he would have trouble with the three participles that described each monster, I also told him that I would read some of the pages. Keith did fairly well with the book and I helped him with single words—*special, set out, rammed, marched, behave, loudest,* and *picked*—throughout the book. I also read the beginning of the second sequence and he took over on *made a mountain rise.* He had trouble with *threw it on the ground.* In several sequences he called *threw* "though," until he read "on the ground" and then he went back and corrected himself. At one point he said, "I keep forgetting it!" In the final sequences I had Keith read the third participle in the participle sequence—*whirling, twirling, swirling and howling, growling, yowling*—and he was able to do it easily. Several times toward the end of the book his reading was labored and I repeated phrases and sentences he had read correctly but slowly to restart him and to help him decode a word on which he had stalled. I have no doubt that if he had read the book the next day he would have read fluently and accurately.

I read several books with Keith that used uncommon sound words like those in *Today I Thought I'd Run Away*. In one patterned book there were lake animals such as frogs and turtles that made sounds like *splish, splash,* and *splosh* when they moved in the water. In another, *Barnyard Animals* (Flemming, 1994), the animals made a variety of noises that were not particularly common and I provided those words to him as well. I found that whenever books used very uncommon words that represented sounds, I usually read them for the child. I also read several challenging books to Keith rather than have him read them himself. This usually happened at the end of a session or after some segment of the lesson proved difficult and Keith seemed to be losing momentum.

As I look over the records of my sessions with Keith and Alan I find that there are many reasons why when I am tutoring I think a particular word phrase or part of a book will be difficult and decide to read those sections to the children. These range from words being phonetically irregular, long, difficult, and not very useful; sound words that probably will not generalize to many stories; and unusual language such as *set off* for *start out*. I also noticed that the emotional tone of the session contributed to my decisions. When sessions were difficult or the child was tired or simply resistant, I did more of the reading in the challenge book.

TRANSITION READER

Transition readers find many books that they can read and they do fairly well in appropriate narrative texts. However, they also are called on to read informative or expository text that makes new and special demands on their reading skills. Recall the session with Mary in Chapter 9. Mary and I were discussing informational books which she explained were, "facts and stuff." We had several books among which to choose. To decide whether she wanted to read the book, she turned to the back cover and read the description. She struggled with the text and stopped midway saying, "I think this is too hard for me." When I asked her what she would do, she answered that she would not read it. However, I pressed her, "Um. If you really wanted to read it what would you do?"

"Well, look through it, or have somebody else read it to me."

I reinforced her strategies by saying, "You might have somebody else read it to you. That'd be a good strategy. Or sometimes if you pair with somebody you can help each other." Then I explained that in books like these (factual books) you do not always have to be able to read the whole thing to be able to read the parts you are interested in. And I began to explore with her how to use the book to get information about a topic she was interested in. We worked with using pictures and captions, skimming the text for hard words, and I explained that she should use understanding as her key. As long as she was understanding the book, it was OK for her to be reading in it.

Transition readers need to be encouraged to use many strategies to determine the meaning of the books they read. Often their challenging books are texts and informational books that they must read for classes to learn basic content. Sometimes the appropriate strategy for dealing with these books is to read them to the child. In fact you may find that transition readers bring books they need help with to tutoring sessions, and it is reasonable for you to spend at least some of the session reading to them. However, most tutors have limited time to spend with the children they tutor. In the area of challenging reading the tutor may be most helpful by being a good advocate for the child with teachers by interpreting the level of the child's reading and making it clear when textbooks are simply beyond the child's ability level. They also may be helpful by working with teachers to make sure that difficult textbooks are available on tape or that the child has access to an assistive reading machine.

FOR THE SUPERVISOR

Helping tutors know when to provide support and when not to is probably the most challenging task for a supervisor. Often beginning tutors who are not skilled at book selection end up choosing difficult books for both the easy-reading and the new-book segments of the lesson. They persist in using the level of support that each segment calls for, and often that level of help is insufficient. The result is the children read poorly and become frustrated. Misjudging early readers' competence is particularly easy and many of them end up with books that they simply cannot read.

First tutors need support to choose books that are appropriate for the various segments of the session. A large portion of initial training should be devoted to exploring books and identifying the elements that make them either easy or difficult for a child. There are several resources that can be very helpful in doing this. One is the Resources section at the end of *Variability Not Disability*, another is *Good Books for Beginning Readers* (Gunning, 1997). This book is useful because it reviews the features that make a book difficult and helps tutors understand how to match children with books. It also has an extensive bibliography that provides brief summaries of many books.

Second, tutors need to learn to recognize the signs of a child's frustration and to evaluate quickly if a mismatch between child and book is causing the problem. When it is a mismatch, they need to learn to switch to the support strategies they use when they are working with challenging books. Simply saying, "Why don't I read the next few pages?" or "Why don't I finish reading?" or "I think this one is a little too hard. Let's try another one," can prevent an imminent disaster.

Chapter 13

Helping Struggling Readers Beyond the Tutoring Session

THE CONSEQUENCES *of learning or not learning to read or struggling to learn to read reach far beyond tutoring sessions.* How we read affects us in many settings and situations. Because of the wide-reaching consequences of reading success and reading failure, it is important to think about what can be done beyond tutoring sessions to help create conditions in which all children learn to read. In the first section of this chapter I will document some of the ways that reading failure may affect children and their families. In the second section I will talk about several ways families, schools, and communities can help create an environment that will allow reading tutoring to have a maximum positive effect.

THE EMOTIONAL COST OF READING DIFFICULTY

Feelings surrounding reading failure are often so difficult that children and families hide their feelings around teachers and other professionals. Talking about reading failure exposes children and their families to a range of responses such as pity, condemnation, and embarrassment that most people would prefer to avoid. To talk about the emotional pain resulting from reading failure is also, in a sense, giving up. Focusing on the pleasure of small successes and the hope that the struggle will end with the child reading is easier than focusing on the failure and leaves parents less vulnerable to the responses listed previously.

Because I work constantly with struggling children and have done so for over 25 years, I have learned to accept the struggles and view them almost as a matter of course. Some children struggle very hard with reading, and I know that behind this struggle lies much pain. This pain was vivid in a set of letters, sent to me by SRP children, their parents, and classmates, in response to my request that they "Tell what it's like in school for children who have trouble reading," so that I could share their thoughts with teachers. (I also have included excerpts from some of these letters in *Variability Not Disability*.) The request went to 15 families who participated in SRP during the same year. In all, I received 21 letters from 10 parents and 8 children.

Some families seemed to have made very positive adjustments to the child's reading difficulty. Jimmy's mother wrote a very positive letter saying that their family is very lucky because Jimmy's reading problem does not really affect them. Jimmy is socially well-adjusted and he is close to his family. They camp, fish, and water ski and the children participate in a variety of sports. His father, a truck driver, takes Jimmy along on a trip once or twice a year. He spells the names of towns so Jimmy can use the map and help him navigate. Jimmy's mother wrote about how Jimmy has adjusted to his problem. She said, "If you never had Jimmy read anything for you, you would not know of his reading problem." And she talked about his awareness that he must listen carefully to make up for his problems with reading. She related the following incident:

> Last year in school the kids were told to put capital letters on proper nouns that were in this list. The teacher read the list out loud pretty fast. She noticed that Jimmy underlined those proper nouns that needed to be capitalized. So after she was done reading the list Jimmy went back and put capital letters on those he had underlined. We have noticed that it is things like this and other ways that Jimmy has picked up that helps him with his reading problem.

Peter's mother also was positive in her writing:

> I think of many things that could be written, the difficulty and the frustrations. First the difficulty in getting help when we first knew our son was different from the norm, the anger in your son's eyes when he wants so badly to be able to do something on his own but cannot due to the difficulty of his reading. The list could go on and on, but of all the suggestions one could make the following stands out. Remember to help them see the many things this person can do. They need badly to see they can succeed. My son at least, works so hard to learn to read and wants to so badly. It's important to show him frequently he has improved. Then also to reassure him and encourage him in the many things he can do well. For example, this last week the Cub Scouts had a fund raising project and he had the top sales.

Randy's mother wrote the following:

I ask myself a lot, "Why Randy?" Randy will never read at a high level. But I still have dreams for him just like I do for my daughters. I know he will make something of his life with a little help from people who care. I believe our kids can do a lot in this world. All kids need help. Ours just need a little more. Our family could not make it without God's help. He is a part of our lives.

She signed the letter, "God Bless You All, Stand By Your Kids."

Tutoring and other forms of intervention do help. For instance, some parents felt that SRP had a made a positive difference for their child. After giving a brief history of Molly's reading development her mother wrote:

This summer after camp Molly *asked* to read books to her youngest sister. Not only that! This year in school they are to do book reports. Well, that did not go over too well until it got started. Then it was fun and at the open house (they chart their books) Molly had read the most in the whole room!

Karen's mother wrote a long letter that detailed Karen's and the family's struggles, but it was a narrative of hope:

Karen is enjoying school the "most ever" this year in fifth grade. Her favorite classes are PE, Art, and Science. She's trying band out and seems enthusiastic. So far she's only negotiated for two "stay at home" days this year. That says it all.

Jamie's foster mother was encouraged by his placement in an SCI room (a special classroom that is self-contained for basic subjects but integrates the children into regular classrooms for some subjects), she wrote:

After the transfer to SCI Jamie became a "different boy." He loved school. His teacher felt that all the kids liked him, and even though he still had problems, so did everyone else. Jamie became more of a leader because he liked helping the other children. Jamie was also selected, as you know, for the SRP program, which was a great benefit to Jamie. We feel his increase in confidence was #1, and of course his acquisition of new reading skills was very evident. Jamie has announced to us: "I am a good reader now and I like to read books." His SCI teacher is considering integrating Jamie with a second-grade reading group. He is in 3rd grade. He certainly still has severe reading problems. We are satisfied with his positive attitude about himself and his reading. He reads to us very often at home and enjoys being read to.

However, several of the letters were anything but hopeful. Holly's mother wrote the following:

I've been putting off writing this letter as it is difficult to express in words my feelings. Most of the time I think I'm living in a never ending roller coaster. We have our highs and our lows—continuously. Life goes on and the struggle to have Holly educated in the best way possible is always before you.

Robby's mother's letter was similar:

This is a really hard letter to write to you because there really is not anything positive to say. Robby does not feel comfortable about reading. It is frustrating for him. We were just talking about writing to you and he made the comment that he wished he was sick so he could stay home instead of reading in his class. We went to the library last week. Instead of going over to the books he is capable of reading he made the comment "they were baby books." Instead he picked out books that had illustrations and were way above his reading skills.

Andy's mother wrote the following:

Our son has a reading problem. He is a healthy handsome child who until this year with all his problems with reading tried his best in school. This year he is nine and in the fourth-grade special education classes. The school has all the Special Ed children together and Andy has to wait for the slowest, he has to watch as some of the really mentally disturbed take hits at the teacher.

I must say I have no positive thoughts when it comes to his education. I have been told, he will be in Special Ed classes for all his school years. I see no bright future for him. I hope to try teaching him at home or try to find a program at a private school. When I think of my son's future in this world, I wish a test would have been given for this problem and I would have had an abortion. I see nothing good for this child in this country and schools for the way nonreaders are treated.

Jason's mother wrote, "I have no funny stories that I can recall to tell, mostly because Jason is a very emotional boy." She then told a story about Jason being embarrassed in front of his classmates by a child who had been asked to correct his test and held up Jason's paper and said he could not read it and that he got them all wrong. She ended with, "I wonder how my child would do if only someone would give him the chance to do it his way instead of making him do it their way."

Regardless of the tone of the letters they all included stories of painful classroom incidents, embarrassments before peers, and unhappiness related to the children's reading difficulties. Jason responded to the incident his mother described by saying, "What am I trying so hard for to do good, when people just laugh at me and call me stupid." Holly tape recorded her letter to me because writing is difficult for her. She talked about putting a cover on her reading book because when she got ready to go home a girl who sat next to her asked to see her reading book. When Holly said no, the girl said, "Why? Because you can't read?" She said it made her feel really sad. When the same girl saw Holly's spelling book and spelling words and said that the words were easy words, Holly lied and said it was not her spelling list. She also reported another incident during the first week of school when she asked a little girl her name and the little girl pointed to the name tag on her desk and said, "Can't you read?"

Jimmy told his mother about a man coming to school to give them a seven-page test and when his teacher asked if she could read it to the children who had trouble reading, the man said no. Jimmy was concerned that the man would think he was stupid.

Andy wrote the following:

> I don't like school this year and I wish I didn't have to go. Lots of kids make fun of me because they know I went to summer school and Special Education Class. I always say to myself I am dumb and hit myself in the head. Sometimes I wish I could die, but my Mom doesn't like to hear that. My Mom and Dad are getting me a computer to help me. I hope next year I can go to a school that will help me.

The children's letters also vary along the dimensions of hope and despair. Figure 22 contains the letters from Jason, Karen, and Randy, all of whom think things are getting better for them. Figure 23 contains a second letter from Jason, one from Peter's school friend, and Peter's "School is hard sometimes" letter.

I have taken the time to give a rather full accounting of these letters because I know of no better way to make the point that the consequences of reading difficulties accompany the child and the child's family through many aspects of their lives. If we are really going to teach every child to read our efforts must go beyond tutoring to creating environments and situations that help classrooms, schools, families, and communities support struggling readers.

MAKING TUTORING PAY OFF

We must create ways for the growth children achieve in tutoring to pay off. Too often in tutoring situations, although children are learning and growing, that growth is simply not enough for them to catch up. As a result their improvement is not recognized and they feel like no matter what they do, it is not enough. What follows are some suggestions for recognizing their achievements both in and out of school.

Use Workshops to Deliver Reading Instruction

Variability Not Disability suggests using a workshop organization to deliver reading instruction in regular school classrooms. The workshop naturally accommodates

Figure 22
The Children's Hopeful Letters

Dear Dr. Roller,
Shool was not eass
when I was in ① + ② grade
It was not eass in 1 + 2 grade
be case no one new adout it—it
as in reading. Now that I am
im 5 grade it is beiter now that
I have had help for 2 summers
in Iowa cite and my mom, teachers
and frints have pelp me.

Ps. I hope I come back
this summer

(continued)

Figure 22
The Children's Hopeful Letters (continued)

Dear Dr Roller Shlool is
Some times hded on me be-
coause I cahnot Read good.
Ih science I took a taset and
chod hot Read it and got
an F but hot anymore.
I in 5 graed ahd the tacr
ord sah myI problm. He
gvis me mor hlpe then a tacr
wahd to a Cild hot like me
bot It is gite btr.

Love
J.C.H.

iTcat foh nox nce ore To red, I wich shis that
i cah red. iT is hot foh, boTi con hot of aI Can rod ned boos
Imn going To a nc s oM.

(Mother's translation: It is not fun not knowing how to read. I wish that I can read. It is not fun. I can read easy books. I'm going to a new school.)

Figure 23
The Less Hopeful Letters

Deer Dr Rollr I falt Defr
from avee One als. pelle
Wror mean to me, and cedd n
bfret from other keens.
I afeef ahle thre tro fres
Aaic Steevn and Lovees.

De or DR Roller
     School is hard Some times.
                    Your Freind

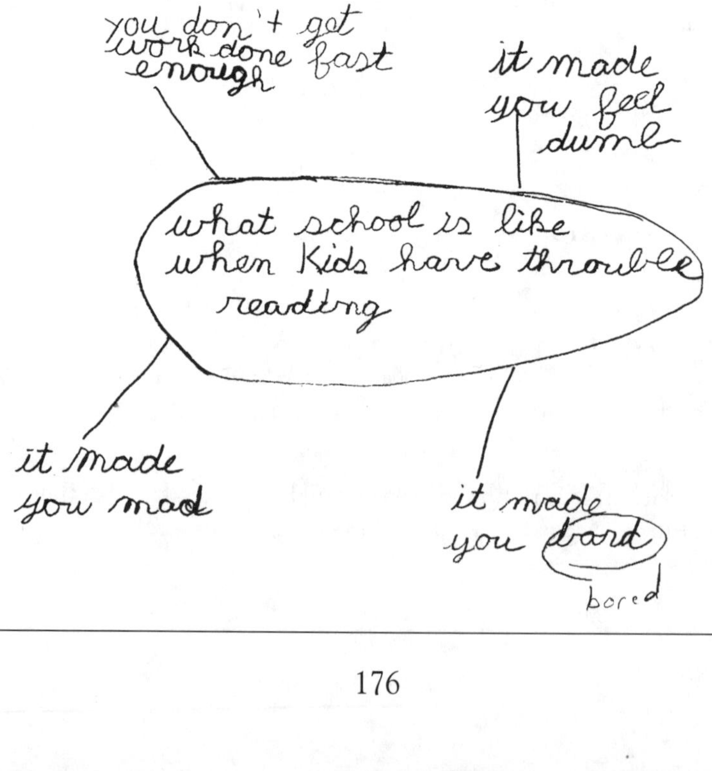

you don't get
work done fast
enough

it made
you feel
dume

what school is like
when Kids have throuble
reading

it made
you mad

it made
you bord
bored

itself to individual differences by allowing children to choose their own reading materials. It is important to understand that workshops are not a technique developed for "special" classrooms and clinical settings. Workshops were developed in regular classrooms, and I learned about workshops from regular classroom teachers. When I set up the SRP workshop classroom I was adapting methods designed for regular classrooms for children who often were not included in them. Workshops allow those who are reading very sophisticated material and those who are reading easy material to participate in the same activities, providing a structure that allows inclusion and differentiation simultaneously.

Workshops are not the solution to all problems and making them work is not easy as those of you who have tried workshops yourselves know. However, workshops are the most sensible way I know to approach classroom reading instruction. Using workshops would go a long way toward creating for all children, the "school that will help me" that Andy hopes for.

Although tutors have little control over how teachers run classrooms (and should not have), the more they are aware of options, the more proactive they can be. It would be appropriate for a tutor to have a conversation with a teacher about workshop classrooms. Workshops are not widely used and some teachers may be unaware of them.

Sharing

Reading must pay off for children in social currency. It helps if their hard work in reading results in praise and positive feedback. If you reflect on the children's letters, you will notice that their frustration is not usually associated simply with not being able to read. It is associated with the social humiliation that results from not being like the other children. Holly was not the only child who wanted to hide her reading book. When Karen went to the library she first would stop at the thick books and randomly choose several. These were to stack on the top and the bottom of the books she really intended to read. She wanted to look like she was reading the same kinds of books as her peers. If you review Chapter 4 of *Variability Not Disability* and Chapter 5 of this book, you will find many suggestions for making easy books acceptable. All of them involve creating ways to share books with other readers in an atmosphere of enjoyment and respect. Sharing is an integral part of workshop classrooms and Chapter 5 of *Variability Not Disability* explains how to organize sharing in classrooms. Whether or not a classroom uses a workshop format however, it always can include sharing by allowing all children time for independent reading and taking a few minutes several times a week for the children to share what they read.

If children do not have opportunities for sharing in their classrooms it is particularly important to incorporate sharing in the tutoring program. At SRP on Tuesdays and Fridays we take the last 20 minutes of the tutoring sessions to gather as a group of tutors, children, and supervisors and share our reading. I find this is a particularly powerful setting for the children to learn effective ways of sharing and responding to books. Because the children are accompanied by their tutors there are many skilled models for children to observe. At SRP our classroom sharing improves when the tutoring groups share because the children seem to pick up so many different strategies from the tutors. Sharing with the tutors present also helps to create a very special and supportive community for the children.

Another important way to provide sharing opportunities is to organize book clubs both within and outside of school classrooms. After-school programs, Boys and Girls Clubs, scouting organizations, church youth programs, and public libraries are ideal places for them. Book clubs for children can work the same way that adult book clubs work—a group of people meet and agree to read a book or series of books and come together and discuss them with one another. With a tutoring program in place, tutors can provide the necessary support for children who have difficulty reading the book selected.

Opportunities for Performance

Another way we can make the gains of tutoring pay off is by providing opportunities for children to show off their reading. Reading to other children and doing Readers Theatre in classrooms, at libraries, in day care and senior centers, and at other community sites are powerful ways to give children social approval for the gains they are making. Some local reading councils affiliated with the International Reading Association organize young readers' conferences, usually on a Saturday. Children from throughout a district will gather at a school, and participate in read-aloud workshops. They bring something with them that they want to read aloud to others and spend a work session with a small group and an adult facilitator to help them polish the reading. Then they move to a performance group and read their stories aloud. At the end of the day all the children gather to hear adult celebrity readers (well-known people from the local community) read.

Incentive Programs

I am very cautious when I talk about incentive programs. I do not think children will become readers because they are given rewards for reading. I believe that if children are to become readers the motivation must come from within, so I do not support giving children certificates, pizza, money, or anything else for reading books. However, that does not mean I do not support incentive programs at all. Incentive programs that use *reading* as the reward can have positive consequences. I would be much more impressed with a promotion that gave children books for eating pizza than I am with a program that gives them pizza for reading books. Likewise, I think rewarding good behavior with books, time for reading, time to listen to someone else reading, or with the privilege of reading to someone are good strategies. What better way is there to communicate that reading is valuable than to assume that it will motivate pizza eating, good behavior, or doing chores?

Family Counseling

Sometimes families get so involved with a child's reading struggles that the child and the struggles threaten to control the family. Everyone worries and everyone suffers. Parents are constantly upset by the daily difficulties and the conversations with school personnel. Often the reading difficulties become emotional difficulties that lead to misbehavior and defiance in school. Parents may fear for the child's future. Will their child drop out of school, get involved in drugs, or be unable to hold a job and take care of himself or herself? When I sense that the family is in turmoil I recommend that they see a family counselor—someone skilled in dealing with the emotional consequences of reading failure. Solving the reading problem is difficult enough when it is not accompanied by emotional upheaval, and it is nearly impossible when it is. A skilled counselor can help defuse the situation. Although reading problems are significant and do often lead to other complications, the problems themselves are not fatal. I have worked with successful adult nonreaders who hold various jobs such as operating heavy equipment, owning a restaurant, and managing a cattle farm. Reading problems can be dealt with and overcome even if the child never learns to read at a functional level. Although I want everyone to learn to read, I want families to know that the world does not become an evil and impossible environment if you cannot read.

FOR THE SUPERVISOR

The ideas suggested here are simply the tip of the iceberg as far as ways to make reading pay off in social currency. Some other possibilities include staging a celebration of the children's reading three or four times a year, taking a group of tutors and children to a day-care center for reading to younger children, having children make tapes of books for children in earlier grades, or doing a special program for parents. This responsibility is one that falls more squarely on the supervisor than it does on the tutor because the supervisor can negotiate for the entire group to create special events, while a single tutor rarely has this kind of power; in addition, if all the tutors are setting up special events it could get very confusing.

Because tutors usually meet with the child one-on-one, they often do not have much contact with the school settings that the child must deal with. The supervisor might want to set up some observation opportunities for the tutors so that they have more first-hand knowledge of what the child's daily school life is like. Rather than visit just their own child's classroom, they should visit the classrooms of several struggling readers so that they begin to develop a deeper sense of the difficulties associated with reading problems.

Tutors also may want to become acquainted with the children's parents. Because parents are often worried about the child's reading, contact with the tutor is important. Supervisors need to spend time training tutors for this contact with parents. I have seen an inexperienced tutor reduce a mother to tears by suggesting she take her son to the library. The mother was already making weekly trips to the library and so far it had not helped. The supervisor must emphasize that parents are to be seen as partners and that assuming that what the parents are doing at home has created the reading problem will not improve the child's situation and is in fact rarely true. The International Reading Association has some pamphlets for parents that will make useful training books for the supervisor.

Chapter 14

Organizing Tutoring Programs

IN THE *Introduction I began by referring to U.S. President Bill Clinton's goal to have every child read independently and well by the end of third grade.* My response to this goal was that if we are going to do this, we should do it right. My fear is that well-intentioned volunteers will develop tutoring programs that actually do as much as harm as good. The notion that every third-grade child will be able to read is somewhat naive and suggests that many of the people involved in this program's conception have little understanding of the complexity of reading development. My first reaction to the America Reads Challenge (ARC) was therefore, "This is really dumb. I do not want to have any part of it!" Obviously, I changed my mind after giving it more serious thought and asking myself, "What would it take to make a program like this work?" What follows is a set of questions we asked ourselves at the University of Iowa and answered as we developed the program.

WHY DID I FIRST THINK ARC WAS DUMB?

I suppose my initial reaction was the result of the over 25 years I have spent working with children who struggle to learn to read. At some basic level I simply do not believe that *every* 8-year-old child can be taught to read "independently and well." There are some children who cannot be taught to talk, walk, dress, or feed themselves. It also may be true that some cannot be taught to read. Although the presence of disabilities does not necessarily mean children cannot be taught to read (remember that physical disabilities do not necessarily mean mental ones), it does mean that teaching *everyone* to read might be very difficult.

But even supposing that the president and his advisors understood that the goal of teaching every child to read was unrealistic, I am still skeptical. I have watched the reading development of many apparently "normal" children over the years. Although some children learn to read on their parents' laps before school begins, sometimes their siblings, who have the same home reading opportunities, do not learn to read after several years of reading instruction in school. Other children struggle to learn although they receive intensive specialized instruction over a period of years. I have seen children who figure out words by themselves and know them instantly forever thereafter. I also have seen children who after 70 exposures to a word still will not recognize it on the 71st try. Reading development is very complex and extremely variable, so my first reaction to ARC was perhaps a bit cynical.

I changed my mind after talking with colleagues, friends, and my husband— mostly my husband—who said, "Why not try it? It is a tremendous opportunity. You may not teach every child to read independently and well by the end of third grade, but if you try, you might help many children learn to read." That made good sense to me. Why not try it? I began to give it serious thought.

ESTABLISHING THE PROGRAM

What does it take to make volunteer tutors effective? My first thought was, "Someone who knows a lot about reading and who has time to devote his or her full attention to the program." I almost quit on ARC right then because I was afraid that the person "who knows a lot about reading" at the University of Iowa would turn out to be me, and I knew that I could not devote even a fraction of the attention it would require to run a good tutoring program. Because the university had received nearly $180,000 dollars to pay work-study students to tutor children in reading, they were very interested in having an ARC program, and they wanted someone from the College of Education to be involved in it. I decided that I would agree to direct the program only if the University committed to hiring at least a three-fourths-time professional staff person with credentials in reading. Because of the work of the Vice President for Student Affairs and his staff, the University made the commitment, we hired a program coordinator, and we began serious planning.

It is absolutely essential to have a professional reading educator in charge of this type of program. After reading this book, you know that learning to read is complex and that tutoring reading is not as simple as sitting down with a child and a book and saying, "sound it out," whenever the child comes to a unknown word. In fact, although this is the most common tactic of untrained individuals, it is usually counterproductive and sometimes quite damaging. Tutors need training and guidance from a professional.

Designing the Tutoring Sessions

As we started the program we had many questions. What kinds of activities could we expect volunteer tutors to do? Should we give them a very structured program? Should we give them printed commercial materials? Should the children read trade books? Should there be worksheets? We decided that the volunteer program should adhere to the same principles we use when training professional reading specialists in our Summer Residential Program. Because reading is complex the best way to teach it is to have the child read real books. We also looked at the kinds of activities included in other successful tutoring programs such as Reading Recovery and Success for All. In these programs most of the tutoring sessions are devoted to having children read. We thus decided on reading easy books, reading the new book, and reading challenging books. We also included writing activities and left some space in the sessions for special instruction to meet specific needs.

We followed the ARC recommendation that tutors meet with students 2 to 3 times a week for at least 30 minutes. We expected to provide about 30 weeks of tutoring over the course of the year—probably 12 weeks during the fall and spring semesters and 6 weeks during the summer. By working with paid work-study students we hoped to avoid, at least until we expanded the program to unpaid volunteers, the problem posed by using volunteers to provide a service that is both intense and must be delivered over an extended period of time. We hoped that many tutors would be able to participate for the entire 30 weeks, but we insisted that the tutors stay with us for an entire semester or summer session. One of the reasons that tutoring is effective is the long-term personal relationship that forms between the child and the tutor. We know that when we begin to expand to community sites and to use more unpaid volunteers we will need to develop some mechanisms for seeing that the volunteers will be able to provide the long-term continuity that is necessary for effective tutoring.

GETTING STARTED

How Did We Recruit the Tutors?

Because our tutors are all work-study students, the work-study personnel at the university played a major role in tutor recruitment. A representative from the student financial aid office visited classes in education in the spring to alert education students to the possibility of tutoring and to encourage them to determine their eligibility for work study. In the summer she notified 3,000 work-study eligible students about the program, and finally we had a booth at the University's annual job fair during the first week of the semester where the program coordinator had a display and an explanation of the program and applications for the position of reading tutor. By October we had hired about 30 tutors.

How Did We Train the Tutors?

We were determined that we would not allow untrained tutors to work with children. Within the ARC Guidelines we were allowed to pay the tutors for reasonable training and planning. During 2 weeks before the tutors went to their sites to tutor we ran training sessions at the times when they normally would be tutoring. These sessions concentrated on acquainting the tutors with children's literature and helping them understand how to provide children with a choice of books that would be at the appropriate level for them to read. We also gave them a few techniques to use when a child encountered an unknown word, emphasizing that the most important response was to give the child time and not jump in too quickly. In addition the tutors read drafts of this book and completed an interactive video presentation on how to tutor. We decided that in the beginning sessions the tutors simply would read with the children in easy books and in just-right books. Because ARC allows tutors time to plan, we decided to do some of the planning in weekly group sessions, and that in the context of planning we could help each of them add to their activities as they were comfortable and the child's needs became more apparent.

How Did We Choose the Tutoring Sites?

There were obviously many possibilities for tutoring sites. Should we run an on-campus after-school program? Should we tutor at schools during the day? Should we tutor in community sites such as churches, libraries, and neighborhood centers? We decided that we would begin at schools—largely because we have good connections in local schools and experience in running practicums and other volunteer efforts in that setting. We worked with school district representatives to plan the program, to develop a short handbook and procedures, and to choose the school sites. The district identified those schools that qualified for federal assistance as the sites where we would begin.

We have a long history of working together with the school district. As a result both we and the school had similar expectations about our respective roles. The University was responsible for recruiting, training, and supervising (as well as paying) the tutors. The district agreed that the advisory board for Volunteer Programs in the Schools, which included school, community, and university representatives, would serve as the advisory board for the America Reads Tutoring Program. The school was responsible for identifying the principal or another staff person as the contact person for the program in the building, identifying and recruiting children, obtaining parent permission, providing space for tutoring and access to the school's library and curriculum lab, and providing a place for tutors to store materials. Tutors are expected to follow regular building procedures for signing in and out.

With a need to get the work-study tutors started, working with the district was the most efficient way to get the program up and running. Organizing new programs is incredibly time consuming and labor intensive and we wanted to take advantage of all the connections we could. However, we hope over the life of the program to expand it to community sites and to involve volunteers as well as work-study students.

How Did We Organize the Tutors?

The feature of our program that most excites me is the way the program coordinator organized the tutors. Three to five tutors visited a school during a particular time. In each of those groups we had at least one student who had more experience and training than the others—usually a student from the College of Education who was involved in an undergraduate teaching program that includes a specialization in reading. These tutors were designated head tutors and were paid a little more. The small groups become a tutoring unit and because the groups were often at the school at the same time and attended the weekly planning sessions together, the head tutors naturally provided leadership. They were very effective in communicating with the coordinator who could then use her time to troubleshoot and solve problems.

Is It Working?

All we can say at this point is "so far, so good!" We are very pleased with the way the program is developing and impressed with the quality and dedication of the people who are tutoring. Informal feedback from the tutors suggests that they like the work and are pleased to be helping the children. As with any new program, there are many details that must be attended to and occasionally one of them is missed, but all the people involved are enthusiastic and so far we have been able to solve the minor problems that have occurred.

Will We Be Able to Sustain It?

We hope that the U.S. Congress will provide the funds to hire reading specialists through the Corporation for Volunteer Service to direct programs like ours and that our application will be funded. As we expand, we hope to be able to apply for Community Block Development Funds and that local service organizations and the United Way will see our program as deserving and give the help we need to continue to provide materials, training, and supervision for the work-study students and the volunteers. We expect the university will continue its support as part of a program to give our undergraduates a chance to do real work in the community.

What Are Our Concerns?

Our biggest concern is what will happen to the children who struggle hardest and who need the most help. Will we contribute to an effort that allows these students to be taught by those tutors who have the least training? I hope not. Because most schools today cannot and do not provide one-on-one tutoring except for perhaps first-grade children in Reading Recovery Programs, I do not see our current tutoring effort as substituting untrained people for professionals. We also target children who are not receiving special support in other school programs.

My hope is that in the long run we will develop a system that allows children who need the most help to have one-on-one tutoring with very skilled professionals. One of the distressing facts about reading difficulty is that for some children (probably about 1% of the population) it takes intensive one-on-one instruction (sometimes several hours a day) over a long period of time (sometimes three or four years) to actually teach them to read. At present only private clinics are able to provide such intensive instruction. Perhaps if early intervention tutoring programs such as Reading Recovery work with many of the children in the lowest 20% and tutoring programs like ours and all those envisioned by ARC provide help to some of the children who just need extra practice and some individual attention, we will be able to use other precious resources to provide the level of instruction necessary for some children to learn to read.

References

Adams, M.J. (1990). *Beginning to read: Thinking and learning about print.* Cambridge, MA: Massachusetts Institute of Technology Press.

Allington, R.L. (1983). The reading instruction provided readers of differing abilities. *The Elementary School Journal, 83,* 548–553.

Baumann, J., & Holman, F. (1996). *Reading challenge—The transition from picture books—Instructional resource.* Athens, GA: National Reading Research Center.

Bransford, J.D., & Johnson, M.K. (1972). Contextual prerequisites for understanding: Some investigation of comprehension and recall. *Journal of Verbal Reasoning and Verbal Behavior, 11,* 719–726.

Calkins, L. (1994). *The art of teaching writing.* Portsmouth, NH: Heinemann.

Chall, J. (1967). *Learning to read: The great debate.* New York: McGraw Hill.

Clay, M.M. (1993). *Reading Recovery: A guidebook for teachers in training.* Portsmouth, NH: Heinemann.

Cohen, P., Kulik, J.A., & Kulik, C.H. (1982). Educational outcomes of tutoring. A meta analysis of findings. *American Educational Research Journal, 19*(2), 237–248.

Crowder, R.G., & Wagner, R.K. (1992). *The psychology of reading: An introduction.* Oxford, England: Oxford University Press.

Eeds, M. (1985). Book words: Using a beginning word list of high frequency words from children's literature K–3. *The Reading Teacher, 38,* 418–423.

Ehri, L.C. (1991). Development of the ability to read words. In R. Barr, M. Kamil, P. Mosenthal, & P.D. Pearson (Eds.), *Handbook of reading research: Volume II* (pp. 383–417). White Plains, NY: Longman.

Fernald, G.M. (1943). *Remedial techniques in basic school subjects.* New York: McGraw-Hill.

Fielding, L.G., Hammons, J., & Janson, J. (1991). *Reading Clinic Manual.* Iowa City, IA: University of Iowa.

Fielding, L.G., & Roller, C.M. (1992). Making difficult books accessible and easy books acceptable. *The Reading Teacher, 45,* 678–685.

Forbes, R., & Roller, C.M. (1991). The relationship of instructional level placement and the informal reading inventory to the process of reading instruction. *Iowa Reading Journal, 4,* 3–9.

Fox, M. (1993). *Radical reflections: Passionate opinions on teaching, learning and living.* San Diego, CA: Harcourt Brace.

Gaskins, I.W., Ehri, L.C., Cress, C., O'Hara, C., & Donnelly, K. (1997). Procedures for word learning: Making discoveries about words. *The Reading Teacher, 50,* 312–327.

Goodman, K. (1996). *What's whole in whole language?* Portsmouth, NH: Heinemann

Gough, P. (1995, April). Paper delivered at Society for Scientific Study of Reading.

Graves, D.H. (1983). *Writing: Teachers and children at work.* Portsmouth, NH: Heinemann.

Gunning, T.J. (1997). *Best books for beginning readers.* Needham Heights, MA: Allyn & Bacon.

Halliday, M.A., & Hasan, R. (1976). *Cohesion in English.* London: Longman.

Handerhan, E. (1990). *Reading instruction as defined by successful teachers and their first grade students in an early intervention program.* Unpublished doctoral dissertation, The Ohio State University, Columbus.

Hansen, J. (1987). *When writers read*. Portsmouth, NH: Heinemann.

Hull, M., & Fox, B. (1997). *Phonics for the teacher of reading: Programmed for self-instruction*. New York: Merrill.

International Reading Association. (1997). *The role of phonics in reading instruction*. Newark, DE: Author.

Johns, J. (1997). *Basic Reading Inventory*. Dubuque, IA: Kendall-Hunt.

Jones, S.B., & Murphy, M.F. (1976). *Geography and world affairs*. Chicago, IL: Rand-McNally

Juel, C. (1996). What makes tutoring effective? *Reading Research Quarterly, 31*, 268–289.

Lewis, C. (1993). Give people a chance. *Language Arts, 70*, 454–461.

May, F. (1997). *Reading as communication*. New York: Prentice Hall.

Morrow, L.M. (1997). *Literacy development in the early years*. Needham Heights, MA.: Allyn & Bacon.

Pearson, P.D., & Johnson, D.D. (1978). *Teaching reading comprehension*. New York: Holt, Rinehart & Winston.

Pressley, M. (1994). *Transactional instruction of reading comprehension strategies*. Washington, DC: U.S. Department of Education, Office of Educational Research and Improvement, Educational Resources Information Center.

Read, C. (1986). *Children's creative spelling*. Boston, MA: Routledge & Kegan.

Roller, C.M. (1994). Teacher-student interaction during oral reading and rereading. *Journal of Reading Behavior, 26*, 191–209.

Roller, C.M. (1996). *Variability not disability: Struggling readers in a workshop classroom*. Newark, DE: International Reading Association.

Smith, F. (1971). *Understanding reading*. New York: Holt, Rinehart & Winston.

Sowers, S. (1984). Six questions teachers ask about invented spelling. In T. Newkirk & N. Atwell (Eds.), *Understanding writing*. Portsmouth, NH: Heinemann.

Stanovich, K.E. (1986). Matthew effects in reading: Some consequences of individual differences in the acquisition of literacy. *Reading Research Quarterly, 21*, 360–407.

Stayter, F.Z., & Allington, R.L. (1991). Fluency and the understanding of texts. *Theory into Practice, 30*, 143–148.

Stroop, D.A. (1935). Lexical access during sentence comprehension: Studies of interference in serial verbal reactions. *Journal of Experimental Psychology, 18*, 643–666.

Sulzby, E. (1985). Children's emergent reading of favorite storybooks. *Reading Research Quarterly, 20*, 458–481.

Sulzby, E. (1986). Kindergartners as writers and readers. In M. Farr (Ed.), *Advances in writing research: Children's early writing, Volume 1*. Norwood, NJ: Ablex.

Topping, K. (1987). Peer tutored paired reading outcome data from ten projects. *Educational Psychology, 7*(2), 133–145.

Wasik, B., & Slavin, R. (1993). Preventing early reading failure with one-to-one tutoring. A review of five programs. *Reading Research Quarterly, 28*, 179–200.

Wilson, C.R., & Hammill, C. (1982). Inferencing and comprehension in ninth-graders reading geography textooks. *Journal of Reading, 35*, 424–428.

Young, C. (1996). *Struggling readers read at a day care center*. Unpublished honors paper, the University of Iowa, Iowa City.

Children's and Adults' Literature References

Arnosky J. (1985). *Watching foxes*. New York: Lothrop, Lee & Shepard.

Asch, F. (1989). *Here comes the cat!* New York: Scholastic.

189

Asbjornsen, P.C. (1973). *The three billy goats gruff*. New York: Seabury Press.

Barrett, J. (1970). *Animals should definitely not wear clothing*. New York: Atheneum.

Brenner, B. (1992). *Beavers beware*. New York: Bantam.

Bridwell, N. (1985) *Clifford goes to Hollywood*. New York: Scholastic.

Brown, R. (1981) *A dark, dark tale*. New York: Dial Press.

Carlstrom, N.W. (1986). *Jesse bear, what will you wear?* New York: Macmillan.

Carroll, L. (1973). *Jabberwocky*. London: Swift Printers.

Cowley, J. (1980a). *Don't you laugh at me*. San Diego, CA: The Wright Group.

Cowley, J. (1980b). *Little red hen*. San Diego, CA: The Wright Group.

Cowley, J. (1980c). *The boogley*. San Diego, CA: The Wright Group.

Cowley, J. (1981). *The bee*. San Diego, CA: The Wright Group.

Cowley, J. (1987). *Mrs. Wishy Washy*. San Diego, CA: The Wright Group.

Cowley, J. (1992). *Come and talk to me*. San Diego, CA: The Wright Group.

Crews, D. (1982). *Harbor*. New York: Greenwillow.

Fleming, D. (1994). *Barnyard banter*. New York: Holt

Galdone, P. (1975). *The little red hen*. New York: Scholastic.

Helprin, M. (1980). *Refiners fire: The life and adventures of Marshall Pearl, a foundling*. San Diego, CA: Harcourt Brace Jovanovich.

Johnson, J. (1985). *Today I thought I'd run away*. New York: E.P. Dutton.

Marshall, J. (1992). *Fox outfoxed*. New York: Dial Books.

Martin., B. Jr. (1983). *Brown bear, brown bear, what do you see?* New York: Holt, Rinehart, and Winston.

Mesler, J. (1990). *If you meet a dragon*. San Diego, CA: The Wright Group.

Most, B. (1990). *The cow that went oink*. San Diego, CA: Harcourt Brace Jovanovich.

Pym, B. (1984). *Some tame gazelle*. New York: Harper & Row.

Randell, B. (1994). *Mushrooms for dinner*. New Zealand: Nelson Price Milburn.

Rey, M., & Rey, H.A. (1986). *Curious George plays baseball*. Boston, MA: Houghton Mifflin.

Seuss, Dr. (1960). *One fish two fish red fish blue fish*. New York: Random House.

Stegner, W. (1961). *Shooting star*. New York: Penguin Books.

Shaw, N. (1986). *Sheep in a jeep*. New York: Houghton Mifflin.

Viorst, J. (1972). *Alexander and the terrible, horrible, no good, very bad day*. New York: Atheneum.

West, C. (1986). *Have you seen the crocodile?* New York: HarperCollins.

Williams, R. (1992a). *I see you*. San Diego, CA: The Wright Group.

Williams, R. (1992b). *Tracks*. San Diego, CA: The Wright Group.

Willis, J. (1987). *The long blue blazer*. New York: E.P. Dutton.

Young, E. (1992). *Seven blind mice*. New York: Philomel Books.

Subject Index

Note: Page numbers followed by an *f* indicate that the reference may be found in a figure; a *t* indicates that the reference may be found in a table.